# THE PORTABLE CREATIVE WRITING WORKSHOP

# THE PORTABLE CREATIVE WRITING WORKSHOP

PAT BORAN

NEW
ISLAND

Copyright © 2005 Pat Boran

THE PORTABLE CREATIVE WRITING WORKSHOP
This edition published 2005
by New Island
2 Brookside
Dundrum Road
Dublin 14

First edition published 1999 by Salmon Publishing

www.newisland.ie

The author has asserted his moral rights.

isbn 1 904301 71 1

British Library Cataloguing in Publication Data.
A CIP catalogue record for this book is available from the British Library.

Typeset by Siobhan Hutson @ Salmon Publishing
Cover design by Fidelma Slattery @ New Island
Printed in Ireland by Betaprint

10 9 8 7 6 5 4 3 2 1

# CONTENTS

WRITING IS ABOUT WRITING; to bea writer is to write. To be a good writer? Well, we'll come to that. For now we just want to get the machinery going. That's what this book is about. If we're actually writing – and not just talking about it – maybe things like technique and form, description and image will make a little more sense. Let's learn by doing or, at least, by trying to do.

But this notion that any of us might just one day decide, 'Hey, I'm going to have a go at that,' is relatively new here in Ireland and further afield. Changing work patterns and increased leisure time for many, coupled with the advent of desktop publishing and global communications, have greatly altered the landscape of writing and the arts in general, but much more than technology is responsible for the huge changes that have occurred since the stifling post-war '50s. Among other factors, the maturation of the women's movment has played an enormous part in what has been effectively a revolution in the arts, providing an organisational blueprint for groups of people of both sexes and from all backgrounds, a blueprint that shows that it's possible to make one's own place in society by connecting to others in similar situations. And the fact is that without this revolution, Irish writing, for instance, might still be obsessed with a handful of dead writers (virtually all of them male) instead of being the vibrant, ever-changing and -evolving organism that, for all its faults, it clearly is.

Among the most prominent features of this revolution was the appearance and spread of creative writing workshops, a kind of forum that seems to have originated in the US but quickly spread further afield, popularised in Ireland by writers such as Eavan Boland. Indeed, it was out of the cauldron of many of these workshops and groups that the first of the new wave of small magazines and independent publishing houses emerged.

But what exactly *is* a creative writing workshop? What goes on, or should go on, in one? Let's start by looking at the ideal.

The ideal creative writing workshop is made up of people of mixed backgrounds, educational histories, sexes, ages, creeds, colours, etc. They come together to share their experience of the challenge of form and technique, along with the occasional moment of insight. In the ideal workshop, people are open with each other, which allows them to make mistakes early on, and often. They learn from their experiments and mistakes and welcome the suggestions and responses of others. This kind of workshop helps all writers, not just those in the group, or even those whose work is under discussion, but even writers elsewhere, distant writers, dead writers, unborn writers. The workshop is a group of people committed to the idea and the craft, the calling and the play of writing.

But this is the ideal, and ideals can be hard to find. The experience of many writers is that the writing group or workshop they attend, while it is beneficial in the beginning, quickly gets itself into a rut. In my own experience, the sense of liberation and support I felt on joining my first workshop was gradually replaced by a feeling that I knew where all this was going, and could sometimes guess what people were going to say even before they said it. And I found myself wishing that someone new would join. What I wanted was outside influence, outside opinion, outside challenge.

This paradox of desiring a group of peers only to want almost immediately to escape from them is the permanent lot of any writer. Those who admire or approve of what we do can often be the people we feel, in the end, are holding us back. And the same is true for our relationships with ourselves. We know we must be writing primarily for ourselves, but which part of myself am I writing for right now? The part of myself I want to be visible to this small group of people who happen to be from my home town? (The Portuguese poet

Fernando Pessoa found a fascinating way around this problem: he wrote poems in four distinct and named voices, leading to what the Irish poet Peter Sirr calls 'an act of self-translation, the fragmentation of his own personality'. Community is something many of us need, but community, where it becomes the dominance of the majority, is unlikely to encourage a writer who feels the urge to mine a vein not considered appropriate to the community's founding ethos. Jean Cocteau advised: 'Listen carefully to first criticisms of your work. Note just what it is about your work the critics don't like – then cultivate it. That's the part of your work that's individual and worth keeping.' And not just critics, but publishers too, can have their blind spots, as Dermot Bolger explains:

> 'Young writers need to look carefully around them at who is publishing what. They need to understand that just because an editor or publisher doesn't like a book or poem it is not necessarily bad. [In 1989] through my then publishing company, Raven Arts Press, I published a wonderful book by Paddy Doyle called *The God Squad*. I tried to sell UK rights to Penguin who at first were very keen. Penguin also took a look at my own novel, *The Journey Home*. Around the same time Transworld publishers asked to see both of these books. Penguin rejected *The God Squad* and published *The Journey Home*, which proved to be a best-seller. Transworld rejected *The Journey Home* and published *The God Squad*, which proved to be an even bigger best-seller. It shows that both publishers had an eye for one best-seller but completely missed out on the other, so that in the end it's down to an editor's personal taste, cop-on and flaws, and you need to keep believing in yourself and plug away. Rejection is not always a bad thing. If Liam Miller's Dolmen Press hadn't rejected Seamus Heaney he might never have been published world-wide by Faber!'

So, a good workshop will at least challenge the writer, and help the writer challenge him- or herself. Even the fact of having to sit there while others discuss the work often gives a writer a real insight into what works and what doesn't, what is actually being expressed and what is being lost somewhere in the process. As Paul Muldoon says:

> 'The most common problem is the one that never goes away. How does one determine what makes sense? It's perfectly clear to the writer, of course. No one else gets it. It's one reason why the person who wrote the poem isn't allowed to speak while it's being discussed, so as not to garble the response of his or her peers.'

## BACK IN 'THE REAL WORLD'

One common remedy for stagnating workshops is to occasionally invite in a visiting writer to 'shake things up'. This visiting writer herself may well be part of a loosely defined group which occasionally needs shaking up: these things are democratic (which is one of the reasons writing workshops terrify some people).

But visiting writers are not always to be found. Like plumbers and electricians, writers asked to share their expertise deserve some form of reimbursement, and such funds are not always available, especially to small groups working outside of the support of a university or arts centre. And, it must be said, some members of a group may be uncomfortable about the idea of inviting in any stranger.

A great many writers simply prefer to work alone. The only group of writers they feel they belong with are those writers whose books line their shelves. For them, no friendly or supportive gatherings in the back rooms of local pubs or community centres. But what then might such individuals, or the members of a small informal group, do to try to bring new energy to their work? In what activities might they engage to feel not only comforted and supported, but also challenged and stimulated?

In my own experience of conducting workshops, it seems to me that many of us could learn something from watching the musicians in our communities and seeing how they pass their time.

As anyone familiar with making music knows, quite apart from the moments and flashes of inspiration, long hours of practice are necessary to prepare the fingers and the heart for the inspiration when it comes, if it comes. In writing circles, most of us will have heard the dictum, 1% inspiration, 99% perspiration. But what exactly are we supposed to be doing to work up that perspiration? If we were musicians we might be playing the scales regularly, practising chord structures and, certainly for most musicians, copying and imitating other musicians. Just as people learn to speak, cook or drive a car by imitation and play, most musicians learn music by imitating others and then playing around with what they have learned to develop new melodies, new rhythms, even whole new ways of playing.

Where many new writers fall, or where many writing groups come unstuck, is where they fail to see how they can develop some kind of training, some kind of system of practice. If one is not inspired to make a poem on a particular day, does that mean that one does not take up a pen or switch on the word processor at all that day? Surely fluency in any art form comes from practice and familiarity?

## MODUS OPERANDI

Your *modus operandi*, or way of working, will be established only by trial and error, but, if possible, err on the working rather than resting side. Samuel Johnson contended: 'A man may write at any time, if he will set himself doggedly to it (and we can only assume he believed that a woman may do the same). Now some of us will find the actual writing a chore, a physical or mental discomfort or even intense pain, while others sail through it like holidaymakers. 'I am a completely horizontal author,' said Truman Capote. 'I can't think unless I'm lying down, either in bed or stretched on a couch and with a cigarette and coffee handy. I've got to be puffing and sipping. As the afternoon wears on, I shift from coffee to mint tea to sherry to martinis.' Other writers go at it in a more determined fashion. 'The best regimen,' according to Lawrence Durrell, 'is to get up early, insult yourself a bit in the shaving mirror, and then pretend you're cutting wood.' Or there's Irish poet Robert Greacen's angle (quoted in *As the Poet Said*): 'Writing poetry is like trying to catch a black cat in a dark room.' If you fail, you could just take it out on your tools. Clarence Budington Kelland, the author of the story which became *Mr Deeds Goes to Town*, had an admirably simple routine: 'I get up in the morning, torture a typewriter until it screams, then stop.'

Between the two extremes of the writer who waits for inspiration and the writer who physically assaults his typewriter come the rest of us. And for most of us, writing is something that has to be accommodated among all the other things we do, whether they be writing related or not. In fact, one of the great things about writing workshops is they allow people to think seriously about writing who may not be, or even wish to be, professional writers. The poet and critic Dennis O'Driscoll, one of many writers who balances a day job and a writing life, has written persuasively of the benefits of having 'a job which is not my vocation'. In a television interview first broadcast in 1998, and collected in his prose volume *Troubled Thoughts, Majestic Dreams*, O'Driscoll considered the relationship between the two:

> '[M]uch as I would love to be allowed to stay home in the ivory tower, it's probably a healthy thing to be shoved out into the grit and grime of the world. You can expand the scope and vocab-

ulary of poetry by bringing to it your long-term experience of worlds and words with which poets are rarely acquainted at first-hand.'

Why we do it, what its ultimate purpose is, and whether we are ever going to be any good at it (and get paid for it), these are impossible questions. But *how* we go about creative writing, about creatively writing, is a question we might well glimpse an answer to if we were to engage in the process.

This handbook attempts to provide some practical direction. The first section of the book, The Raw Material, deals with ways to help generate material for future revision, and the methods and approaches contained in it are the kind of thing I suppose I hoped some visiting writer might bring to my own first workshop. The second and third sections concentrate on poetry and fiction respectively.

Throughout the book I use the word 'games' rather than 'exercises' when discussing methods of drafting and revising material, not because I think the process is something less than serious (on the contrary, it can be very serious indeed), but because I think the word games reminds us that, like musicians, much of what we learn we learn through play. Indeed, many of us will resist at some level those activities that we perceive to be overtly about learning, possibly because of bad learning experiences when we were younger. Therefore, to give the book any chance of emulating even some of the effects of a living writing workshop requires a certain kind of focus from its readers, that 'willing suspension of disbelief' any book asks for. But it also asks readers to bring to their writing a willingness to make mistakes and to recognise them as such. It's somehow easier to recognise you've made a mistake when you're exposed in front of a group of your peers; it's a little more difficult at home in your room where everything you write seems either great or terrible.

Publication may or may not follow and rewards may be scarce. Most of us will never need to worry about Larry L King's advice to young writers: 'Get all the money in front of you and check the cash quickly.' No creative writing hand-book should get involved in making promises of wealth and fame (though some of them do), as no good music teacher should push all her pupils towards the National Concert Hall. Some of us will publish books and others will not, just as some of us will drive in Formula 1 and others will just drive occasionally to the local supermarket. The real point is that being a writer means engaging with writing and reading. It means exploring and getting lost, being certain and not having a clue. You give words access to your life, outer and inner, and you give your life, outer and inner, access to words. For this reason, any community of writers should also be a community of readers. But this is not always the case. Here's Irish poet Paula Meehan on the same subject (talking in particular of poetry, but the same might be applied to fiction):

> 'Too narrow a range of reading is the most common obstacle I come across in poetry workshops. The stronger a reader you become, in depth as well as breadth, the better chance you stand of not re-inventing the wheel. Sometimes a beginner is writing a poem whose audience is already dead. They might even be writing a perfect 19th century poem. To write for the living is the work; or to be one of those rare visionaries who is writing to the future. Other than that I think "problems" are the areas where real growth happens for a poet. It is what is fractured, problematic, unresolved, in the language and the life that energises poems. It is at the edge of what we can't say, yet have to find the language for, that the poem begins.'

To find that language we have to travel in as well as out. We have to discover things within ourselves and we have to touch and weigh and measure the things of the world. And no one can expect an easy ride, as Theo Dorgan warns in *Irish Poetry Since Kavanagh*:

'Bad poets set themselves low standards, good poets aim for high standards, and the ruthless muses of memory and history tend to the preservation of a fraction only of the good.'

For myself I have to say that there is always too the chance that all of my own work, my own poems and stories, will come to mean nothing, and that my real part in the 'revolution' will have been to say the right word, to offer just the right amount of support or challenge or direction when and where it was needed. Hence my own interest in writing this book. I might have been born in the Middle Ages, or in the twentieth century in a country where writers are persecuted, tortured, murdered for doing what they do. Ken Saro-Wiwa in Nigeria in 1996 was one such writer. Salman Rushdie very nearly was one. And there are hundreds of others. After the revolution in her own country toppled the former Communist regime, the Romanian poet Daniela Crasnaru said: 'Now we are able to use all the words in the vocabulary.' In the 'free west' we already have all the words in the vocabulary at our disposal, but do we really appreciate them? Saul Bellow said: 'Poets have to dream, and dreaming in America is no cinch,' but in fact that kind of dreaming is becoming more difficult everywhere. And as anyone who has ever told a dream in company will realise, dreams prompt other dreams, just as poems prompt other poems, and stories other stories. And so it continues. Personally, I'd like to do something to help ensure that the 'revolution' during which I was lucky enough to be born will continue after me. Irrepressible. Irresistible. Unpredictable.

In his thought-provoking and eminently useful little book, *Today You Are My Favorite Poet: Writing Poems with Teenagers*, American poet and teacher Geof Hewitt includes a game designed to get a classroom full of teenagers to collaborate on the writing of a poem. With no explanation of the purpose of the exercise, and certainly no mention of poetry beforehand, each teenager is asked simply to write down a single line or even just a phrase, something that passed through their minds earlier that day, something heard, read, remembered, and then all the lines and phrases are written down on the blackboard, one under the other, as if they were all along the lines of a free verse poem. To derive more than just a few moments of entertainment from the accidental juxtapositions, Hewitt then invites the students to edit and rewrite the poem, keeping faithful to the 'original' as much as possible but exercising the freedom to add linking phrases, chop away distractions and inconsistencies, to come up with something which, for all its strangeness, might read as if it had been written by a single person, from a single point of view.

I've tried this game, and versions of it, many times and in many different situations, and what strikes me most about it, and seems to strike the players themselves, whoever they are, whatever their age or background, is just how potent and magical and ALIVE language is when we give it our undivided attention. Even language that belongs to no single one of us seems to belong to us all.

Trusting that I've made my point – experiment! fail! read! – let's go on to the first section of the book proper, the part intended to help us loosen up, to help us get things down, in whatever shape or form, to give a glimpse into our possibly hidden inner resources.

# *The*

# *Raw Material*

'WRITING IS EASY,' for American journalist and biographer Gene Fowler. 'All you do is sit staring at a blank sheet of paper until the drops of blood form on your forehead.' But maybe that's not the only way, at least not all the time. In this first section of the book, we're going to start, as anyone should before playing what may well prove to be strenuous games, by warming up. In the second and third sections we'll look at aspects of poetry and fiction in detail; in this first section we'll try to leave those categories to one side and instead just work at producing 'pieces of writing'. For some of us, a number of these may well develop into poems, or stories, but what we're really interested in here is freeing up the process, stretching ourselves a little, getting some exercise. And the less we think about categories like poem and story, the less preconceived ideas of what they might be we'll be carrying with us as we go. That's the theory anyway. The reader who wants to get the most from this book will go slowly through the first section before moving on to either or both of the other two, and ideally things in this first section will be returned to every now and again. Many of the games (or exercises) described here only begin to pay off if they are practised on a regular basis.

# LEARNING TO LEARN

All learning activities work as follows: you begin knowing nothing, you move on to a recognition of the rules, then to the *learning* of the rules (or rules of thumb, almost literally), and then you're there. At first the rules seem constricting, even arbitrary. *Who made these damned rules anyway?* Then you start to notice that some of the rules work, and you get a little excited. Until you realise that there are dozens, hundreds, thousands of rules. This is a difficult period, the period where the musician must over and over practise her scales or the athlete must swing for hours on the parallel bars. This is the part where all our logic and concentration come into play, and the part where most of us get bogged down and from which we never advance.

However, if this period is given due attention, it is followed by a period during which the rules are gradually absorbed, and the person re-experiences the freedom he knew before awareness of the rules proved a distraction. He is playing again, with the obvious difference that he is now more aware of what it is he is taking on.

Take the example of the person who decides to learn to drive. The first few efforts in the driving seat are hopeless, maybe even terrifying. With enormous conscious effort the beginner driver tries to perfect the timing and manipulation of peddles, gears and brakes, lights, horn and indicators, not to mention steering wheel! (Accelerator, Brake, Clutch ... He's gone all the way back again to his ABC.) So he drives like that, like someone struggling with a metal contraption designed to get him along the road. He might even hit the odd thing now and again: the footpath, the corner of the gate, a parking cone. And then one day, he finds himself miles from his home. He has driven there. And he has done it with little or no conscious effort.

Now somewhere between his early over-consciousness and his later no-consciousness there's a good driver. In his *The Use of Lateral Thinking*, Edward de Bono has the following to say on this relationship between play and learning:

'During play ideas suggest themselves and then breed further ideas. The ideas do not follow one another in a logical progression, but if the mind makes no attempt to direct ideas and is curious enough to pursue them there will always be enough ideas – often there will be too many. The ideas may not prove useful immediately, but have a habit of turning up later. Even if no specific idea turns up, the general familiarity with a situation which is provided by playing around can prove a most useful background for the development of further ideas.'

For creative writing, as for most other things, practice is the only way to stay in form and very often, even from games and distractions such as those that follow, the great elusive idea you've been searching out for years rears its head. All the ideas in the world won't make a poem or story. Very often, the only way to make either is to be writing when the idea comes. As one of my favourite poets, Robert Frost, said, 'A poem is an idea caught in the act of dawning.' And in many ways, the joys of creative writing are the accidents that happen when you are as prepared for them as you can be.

## PLEASURABLE EXPERIENCE

'I agree to like you. Let's forget that argument we had earlier where you stole my girlfriend.' A conversation that begins like this is unlikely to stay healthy for very long. Similarly, statements of intent about art or music or poetry are of little real use. Unless, of course, they are quickly followed up with some kind of experience. Obviously a good experience induces in us a desire to undergo further periods of the exprience, while a negative one has the opposite effect (remember Pavlov's dogs?)

A pleasurable experience is necessary if we're to keep up our interest, if we're to reawaken our own sense of experimentation. And the best way to guarantee a pleasurable experience is to allow ourselves in advance to fail, to screw up, to make a mess of things. I'm not a very good guitar player, but if I don't allow myself to make mistakes how can I ever improve? So I screw up, and enjoy screwing up in a way, and sometimes even get something right by accident. But a funny thing about that kind of accident is it only ever happens *when* I am playing the guitar. When I *think* about it, or *talk* about it, nothing happens. I have to be actually doing it to learn. I learn to do, and do in order to learn.

The same is true of writing. If we want to learn something about the process and about ourselves, we actually have to write. While most of the games in this book have a pretty definite purpose, for many of us the material we produce will not seem to match our expectations or what we imagine are the author's expectations. But this simply doesn't matter. If the book should impart any one thing it is that there is no one correct way to go about writing, and that instead we all find our own way there or not. The games described in this book are simply some suggestions as to how we might kick-start various aspects of the creative act.

# AUTOMATIC WRITING

*Write what you know.* That's the advice all would-be writers are given. But sometimes, particularly when you're hunting for a new idea, or feeling that you've run into a wall on the old one, it's better to write what you *don't know*, and not as difficult an undertaking as it might at first sound. If, as Oscar Wilde suggested, 'All bad poetry springs from genuine feeling,' and maybe even all bad writing, we'll try instead for what WH Auden called 'the clear expression of mixed feelings'. We'll try to make things clear and concrete and appealing to the senses (sight, touch, taste, smell, hearing), even if we don't yet know quite what we mean.

My first meeting with the poet, novelist and publisher John F Deane was on a writing course back in 1986 where he was one of the visiting tutors. The thing I remember about his workshop was when, after reading a series of quiet and very moving elegies to his late wife, he answered a question on how he finds the quietness within himself to write by saying (and I paraphrase): 'Sometimes I turn the sound on the television all the way up so I can't think.' If what we're trying to do when we write poems is discover something within ourselves, it might be that our best chance of doing so comes when we are absorbed or distracted by something else. Once our guards are down, the raw material that may be emotion or insight or imagination often finds its way to the surface.

But how do we do this, and how do we know it works? Well, let's answer the second question first. We know it works because we know lots of writers have approached writing in this way at one time or another. Yeats is perhaps the most famous example. What opium and drink were to Coleridge and Dylan Thomas, by times the occult, automatic writing and divination were to him. But what makes Yeats so interesting for us is that, while he played with ouija boards and automatic writing, he also knew the importance of form. 'Irish poets, learn your trade. / Sing whatever is well made,' he wrote, and he also answered the question of how he made poems by saying that he was looking for the next rhyme, a process at once automatic *and* craft-based.

And we know that it is not only writers who have taken the idea of automatic writing seriously; so too have those who would like to control the way writers think and work. Though it hardly rates as great literature (which is a word you won't find too often in this book), the words of the throwaway pop song 'Louie Louie', generated in this manner, occasioned a secret FBI investigation when the ultra right-wing J Edgar Hoover decided the song might be an attack on the American Way. In other words, automatic writing is a powerful force, and one that has been accorded both respect and fear throughout history. Speaking in tongues, for instance, is a version of it and, depending on where and when you lived historically, might have seen you either hailed as a prophet or condemned to death as a witch.

But automatic writing and speaking in tongues is not just an artistic adventure. Lovers engage in a form of it when they use pet words and expressions for each other; children engage in it all the time. The exhausted, the drunk, the emotionally challenged, all have recourse to it.

Now that we know what it is, how do we get started?

---

Take a pen and paper, or switch on your computer, and, setting yourself a time limit of no more than five minutes, write the first thing, and any subsequent thing, that comes into your head. Imagine you're drunk, imagine you're dreaming, imagine you're insane. The point is to write as fast as you can so that you don't start to think or worry about what it is you're writing. For once, you are interested in quantity rather than quality. You simply want to write as much as you can, as fast as you can, in the allocated five minutes. And like John F Deane, if you like you can always turn up the television or the radio to full volume, or you can go and sit in the middle of a noisy cafe. For the next five minutes you are opening the floodgates.

---

We'll be returning to versions of the automatic game throughout this book (the poetry section features an extended version of the game, intended to steer us towards something like the material for a poem). For the moment, however, just concentrate on letting go, on getting used to the feel of writing without direction, on surprising yourself. Play this game a number of times until you feel relatively comfortable with it. Then we'll look at a subtly different version.

# GUIDED AUTOMATIC WRITING

Guided automatic writing differs from automatic writing in that before we begin to write we pre-select an opening phrase with which to commence. The disadvantage of this approach is that this opening phrase, no matter how innocuous it may seem, obviously steers our automatic flow in a particular direction, which might not always be what we want. The advantage, on the other hand, is that it sometimes helps to have somewhere to begin, especially if we are in the earlier stages of automatic writing and still tend to worry about whether or not we will come up with anything useful.

The American poet Deena Metzger in her wonderful book on creative writing, *Writing for Your Life*, suggests beginning with a phrase like 'He appeared ...' and continuing the automatic writing from there. A phrase like this can be very useful indeed to kick-start the process, and Metzger's is especially helpful for the way in which it embraces action (appeared) and mystery (he – who is he?) Like all good openings it catches our attention and at the same time prompts us to ask questions. And, of course, 'she appeared' or 'they appeared' or even 'it appeared' do more or less the same thing.

When choosing an opening phrase, then, it's important to choose something that is not static but that leads into something more to come. One good way of finding opening phrases like this – and remember we are using the phrases only to get started, after which we can delete or modify them as we please – is to look at the openings of other stories or poems or even newspaper articles. Somebody said that all poems are responses to other poems, and in the same way every time we write, at some level, we are responding to other writing or language, so by choosing an opening phrase we get to cut straight to the centre of this response process. (For this reason, it is often very helpful to have a dictionary of quotations to hand, as somewhere in it there are bound to be a few words or sentences which will immediately spark off some kind of response in you. But more of this later.)

17

The final thing to say here is that it's important not to worry too much about what comes as a response to the opening. If we find a sad poem or story that begins 'He appeared ...', for the purposes of this exercise at least there is no pressure to continue either in the same mood or on the same topic. In fact, ideally, once we have written down this opening phrase we should be trying to let the floodgates of language open up so that we are too busy writing down whatever comes to worry about what it means or how faithful or unfaithful it may be to the original opening. As with the earlier version of automatic writing, the point is to generate raw material, quantity not quality, and worrying about things like this at this stage is really just your Inner Critic saying, 'This is no good. I told you this was going to be no good,' or whatever his stock put-downs are.

> ✍
>
> Take a phrase from a poem or story or newspaper article, preferably one which includes elements of action and/or mystery, and use it as the basis from which to begin automatic writing for five minutes.

## A–Z

The A–Z free writing game is one of the least promising but most surprising of short games that can be dashed off in a few minutes. As with the automatic writing games described earlier, the point here is simply to complete the game as quickly as possible and then to go back at a more leisurely pace and see what, if anything, might prove to be of use. In a sense, then, this game also comes in two parts.

As far as the rules go, there really couldn't be anything simpler. As the English language uses 26 letters to represent itself, we'll first use these 26 letters to suggest free associations and then see where these associations lead us. To begin, it might be helpful to write the alphabet across the top of the page you're working on. This way a quick glance up at any time will be enough to remind you of where you are and what is expected next without interrupting the flow. Again, as with the automatic writing games, any pause at all here will make what should be an entertaining game into either complete nonsense or the most impossible challenge of your writing life.

This is how it goes: with the 26 letters written across the top of the page, you are now going to write a total of 26 words, no more and no less, each beginning with successive letters of the alphabet, the first word beginning with A and the last beginning with Z. Rather than just compose a list of 26 things beginning with the 26 letters, however, the challenge of this quick game is to write in grammatical English sentences, or to at least try. By putting these two constraints on the game, there is some chance at least that the finished product will contain accidental and hopefully fortuitous meanings and suggestions which can be used later on.

Just to make this absolutely clear, and at the same time not wishing to steer you too much in my direction with examples, I'll show you a couple of the millions of possible openings that might spring up. Remembering that the first word must begin with A and the second with B and so on, here they are.

1. A Black Cloud Drifted Eastwards. etc.
2. Angels Began Crying. Death Ends Fear. etc.
3. After Birth Cells Divide Every Few etc.

As you can see from the examples above, the length of the sentences you make from the 26 given beginning letters is not what matters. In the first example the first sentence is five words long, in the second it's only three and in the third it's already six words long and still going. Sometimes you find yourself on a 'roll' where you can use six, seven, eight or more letters all in the one sentence and sometimes sentences come in just two or three. You must remember, though, to keep the game challenging, that you have to make English sentences but that you can, of course, punctuate them whatever way you like. By the time you get towards the end of the alphabet, down to W, X, Y and Z, it tends to become pretty difficult to keep the game going, but don't worry about this. Xylophone and Zebra might be the only words that strike you when you come to X and Z, but even so try to make the most of the letters that came before and push the sense of meaning out as far as you can. The finished piece of writing, consisting of 26 words, may not make a whole lot of sense to you, even if you have somehow managed to keep a thread of narrative throughout, but, as with the automatic writing, it should bring up some interesting lines and phrases of its own. And if all this seems just too difficult for you, you can always bend the rules a bit and allow yourself to use proper nouns (the names of persons or places) to expand the possibilities.

1.  Aunt Beatrice Came Driving Every Friday. etc.
2.  Amazingly, Barry Carthy Drank Ethanol! Four Gallons! etc.

If it's at all possible, though, try to keep the use of names to a minimum. What we're looking for here are phrases that stand alone as interesting or unusual. We're looking for concise pieces of raw material that we can play with and reshape later.

*

A second, optional part of this game, which might particularly appeal to fiction writers, is to then take the finished piece of A–Z writing and rewrite it, giving yourself room to expand on ideas and images that came up and an opportunity to clarify aspects of the narrative.

# THE LIVING ROOM

What you notice, what you recall from a particular situation and how you then choose to describe it tells a lot about the kind of person you are. When a group of art students, for example, are sat around a vase and asked to paint what they see, the same vase of flowers comes out subtly or radically different on their equally sized canvases, even if an art teacher is present looking for some kind of similarity. The depictions of the flowers differ, not just because the flowers somehow keep changing (which of course they do; the light changes in the room, a petal may fall off, etc.), but also because the people who paint them are different: they see the flowers differently. What they paint and how they paint it illustrates these differences.

Objects for the creative writer provide what we might call possible doorways to the inner self, in that if we could record our own or our characters' reactions to them we would be giving a glimpse into the often hidden world of feeling. Of course, objects are also doorways to other times and places. Bringing as they do a history of their making with them, they might also reward the kind of attention which looks for not only a glimpse into its own interior but also a glimpse into the bigger story, the bigger picture of humankind. In a short essay entitled *Some Thoughts on Impure Poetry*, the Chilean poet Pablo Neruda (around whom the film *Il Postino* is loosely based) discussed this very matter.

> 'It is worth one's while, at certain hours of the day or night, to scrutinise useful objects in repose: wheels that have rolled across long, dusty distances with their enormous loads of crops or ore, charcoal sacks, barrels, baskets, the hafts and handles of carpenters' tools. The contact these objects have had with man and earth may serve as a valuable lesson to a tortured lyric poet. Worn surfaces, the wear inflicted by human hands, the

sometimes tragic, always pathetic, emanations
from these objects give reality a magnetism that
should not be scorned.'

Interestingly, Anton Chekov gave very similar advice:

'To a chemist, nothing on earth is unclean. A
writer must be as objective as a chemist; he must
abandon the subjective line; he must know that
dungheaps play a very respectable part in a
landscape, and that evil passions are as inherent in
life as good ones.'

If we were to follow this kind of lead then, whether we are
ultimately attracted to poetry or fiction, it might be interesting
to see what a meditation on some common, even household,
object might produce.

Take some object with which you are so familiar
that most of the time you pay it no real attention.
How does it differ from all other similar objects
you've known and in what ways is it the same?
Study it with all your senses. Describe its colour, its
texture, its feel. Feel its weight. Where is the object
bringing you? As a painter might try to capture a
bowl of fruit or a vase of flowers in paint, try to
capture the object in words.

When you've written a page or so on your object, look back
over what you've written to see which elements of the
description most capture the reality of it for you? Do those elements include material that invokes the senses (sight, touch,
taste, smell, hearing)? What do the words you have used to
describe the object (big, blue, heavy, cracked, etc.) suggest on

their own when you forget for a moment you are just dealing with this object. And, though we'll examine symbol later in more detail, what might that object as you have described it suggest or symbolise if you were writing a story about a lonely man whose only possession was this object or, alternatively, a poem about desire whose only concrete image was the object?

Though there are many ways to approach a game like this, just to give you one example of how you might proceed, here's a poem of my own called 'Penknife' which came out of just such a meditation.

> *Penknife*
>
> Still smelling of oranges
> after years in this drawer
> among buttons, paper clips,
> envelopes, old specs ...
>
> a present from you,
> designed to sever,
> it's the one thing
> that somehow connects.

While I don't mean to suggest that this is the best or only way of approaching the exercise, one can see how the detail selected to describe the penknife (its smell), perhaps because it was not the first or only detail to be considered, eventually led me out into the bigger picture, the bigger story of relationships. Again Edward de Bono makes a strong point about this notion of relationships and play. 'Play is an opportunity,' he says, 'to try out and test new relationships. It is also an opportunity to become aware of relationships that come about by chance.'

Similarly, alongside the penknife itself, all the other objects mentioned in this short poem, in some way, deal with relationships: buttons hold things together, as do paper clips; envelopes contain things; spectacles connect the viewer to the object of vision, etc. Once the penknife and the other objects in the poem are allowed to function, and not just sit there lifelessly, they lead almost inevitably to the conclusion of the poem so that the poem itself becomes a short meditation on relationships and connection.

## INNER FIGURES

Every time each one of us sits down to write, we sit down not only in the company of other writers but also in the company of a host of what we might call our own Inner Figures. These Inner Figures are made up of all our experiences of writers and writing, our received opinions about what makes a writer or what makes a good piece of writing and our hopes and fears for ourselves as writers. Some of these received opinions and ideas may well be what has brought us to wanting to write in the first place, but many of them may well be the very things which hold us back. For some of us, every time we sit down to write one of these Inner Figures says, *Hey, This is fantastic! Everything you write is fantastic!* And then, two minutes later, or after the first draft has been completed, another one pipes up with, *Who are you kidding? This is just rubbish like everything else you write.* Who do we listen to?

Obviously, if we hope to spend a lot of time writing, and time is something we must be prepared to spend, we need to find ways of dealing with these Inner Figures. One possibility might be to personify them, to deal with them as if they were real individual characters and to try to get them into some form of dialogue to see what it is they want, what they are afraid of, how they might be persuaded to be helpful rather than a hindrance.

In this section, then, we will look at four of these Inner Figures: the Poet, the Shadow, the Critic and the Guide. Though four, in a sense, is an arbitrary number (sometimes the qualities and characteristics of these Inner Figures overlap or are common to more than one), by trying to deal with them as individuals we have a better chance of finding out what it is that makes them tick. Let's start with the first of these Inner Figures, the one we might call the Poet.

## NO. 1 – THE POET

Ironic as it may seem, for all creative people one of the biggest obstacles that stands in the way of creation is the Poet, the Musician, the Artist inside each one of us. By this I do not mean the natural creative spirit we all possess and which is developed in us to varying degrees. Instead I mean that (often inaccurate) *image* of the Poet, the Musician or the Artist that each of us carries within, an image shaped by our schooling, our communities, etc. (Possibly because of an unfortunate bias against *doing* in most educational systems, many of us are left with unsound stereotypes which keep art and artists at one remove from our real lives.) My own Poet, for instance, who has been with me since I was about seven, is late middle-aged, bearded (he is male 99.9% of the time), is usually dressed in cardigan and slippers and can often be found out on the hills at the back of his mansion – in which, of course, he insists on living in the dreary and damp attic surrounded by dusty tomes – butterfly net in hand swirling through the air. His favourite words are *yonder, o'er* and *verily.* (He dismisses the notion that Shakespeare was writing in the language of his own time, and misses the point that the challenge is to make poems out of our own language, to make the extraordinary out of the ordinary. As someone – I'm afraid I can't remember who – wrote: *If every generation wrote with the voice it knew from the past, contemporary poetry would still be in the style of Chaucer and Shakespeare;* but this is a point lost on my inner Poet.) On bad days, for instance, he may be found with a bottle of whiskey in front of him, a cigarette burning his lips and smarting his eyes. On these occasions his favourite words in the dictionary are of Latin origin and tend towards abstraction:

isolation, dehumanisation, desolation. This Poet is based on all the half-digested images of poets (almost all male again) from my early schooling. This permanently insightful, soulful, sensitive – sometimes to the point of melancholia – being sits down beside me every time he hears me think the word poem, every time I begin to write.

I am still in the process of developing the rules of a game with him to relieve him of his dominant impotence. It would not be good enough for me to simply dismiss him as irrelevant, for then I would be unprepared for how he might reassert himself at some later point. (This very thing has happened to an acquaintance who began by writing radical and impulsively spirited poems and then suddenly was confronted by the archetype of the powerless, preening poet, the sensitive soul-searching loner, and his writing just as suddenly stopped. What he needed to do was take on board some kind of engagement game for this other half.)

There is also the deep suspicion that not all of what the Poet has to say can be so easily dismissed. The fact that poems can and often do contain feelings of sadness and loss is something I must be careful not to forget in my dealing with him, for without this knowledge, this permission, I am lessening myself in trying to be free of his influence. I am replacing one stereotype with another, but I have yet to begin living and feeling for myself. In my desire to create poems that have my own sense of humour, my own footprints through them, I must be careful to examine his views and his responses one by one. The 'I' I am willing or able to recognise at any particular time may not be the whole me, and certainly not the whole potential me.

In my struggle with and against this voice, this Poet, I have developed the following game. It is perhaps not an uncommon game – in fact, its simplicity is reflected in many forms in many cultures – but the version I use has been adapted to fit into the life I've led and the experiences I've had. (This is another thing about games: do not be afraid to adapt them to suit your needs.) In my version of the game, anyway, what I do is I sit down on a regular basis – depending on my working habit at a particular period – and before I begin to write what I think is on my mind, what I want to write, I write something completely different. Often this something is quite trivial, maybe a shopping list, a letter of praise or complaint about a radio programme, a still-life portrait of some object in the room. In doing so, however, I allow one or other of the Poet's personalities completely free reign –*yonders* everywhere, clouds of cigarette smoke billowing in the imaginary room, all the melancholia in the world. Then I stop, maybe make tea or walk around the room, come back and read it and with everything that is extreme and clichéd exposed, manage, if sometimes only for an instant, to write like myself.

Writing like yourself is not as easy as it sounds (especially if your Poet, or Novelist or Dramatist, has opinions as trenchant as does mine). It doesn't mean, for instance, that simply by *wanting* to be yourself you immediately are. The self is made up of what appear to us to be many different parts, and some of these are not only out of contact with others, but even exist without our ever being aware of them. The process of improving at something like the writing of poems or stories or the painting of pictures, or even the typing of business accounts, is the process of becoming conscious of and enlisting the most productive parts of these various aspects of the self. Even a book which suggests games to enable this process to be continued within the reader has itself to be played with as a game and should not be taken on face value.

This is not to say that what is in the book is useless (I sincerely hope it isn't); it is simply to remind us that knowledge is not the same thing as wisdom: it is merely one of the ingredients, the other major one being experience. While there is nothing in this book I feel has not earned its place (if it was worthwhile and enjoyable for me, then I suspect it might be for others), and while I pass it on in good faith, none of it can mean anything or should be prized unless it is tested by the reader's experience.

How seriously one decides to measure the usefulness of

games is a personal matter. On a scale of one to ten, some people will invest only three in the playing of a particular game; others will perhaps go as close as eight or nine. Total commitment to a game with a pen and a piece of paper, when there are no Lottery millions at the end, no champagne, no cuddly toy, name in the frame or score on the door, is difficult. The only way to overcome this difficulty is to decide straight away that one will play the game at level ten right through, no matter how silly it might seem, that one will prepare for the silliness or embarrassment by jumping in now at the deep end, the shallow end, the end which is nearest in any given moment.

### The World's 'Worst' Poem

Write what you think is the worst poem or short piece of fiction you've ever read. Bring in all those hackneyed, clichéd expressions you can muster. Write it in that form that you have always felt was dead and boring. Rhyme (badly) all over the place, or spend an inordinately long time describing your heroine's eyes as if she had not other parts to her body. Don't just make it bad, make it terrible. And then put it to one side and write something good. And then ask yourself: why is the second piece better than the first? Are there any points of similarity between the two? Are there any good things at all in that first version? If you were now to imagine removing all the stuff you think is rubbish, is there any glimpse there of something interesting being said?

## NO. 2 – THE SHADOW

As an Inner Figure, the Shadow is a fairly powerful one whose name gives us a good idea of his function. What the Shadow wants more than anything is to keep things hidden, things we don't like about ourselves, or even things we do. (For some people the problem of writing is coming to terms with the possibility that they might actually be good at it!)

Whether your shadow is in front of you or behind you or hiding under your feet, the first step towards finding him/her is to find a light, for where light exists shadows can't be far behind. To find our psychic shadow, if we can call it that, the first step is to find the psychic light. To do this honestly and with anything like clarity may feel like an insurmountable problem. Like trying to describe the universe while we are still inside it, trying to describe ourselves is, at best, a subjective exercise.

One possible way around this problem is the list. To begin the Finding Your Shadow game we are going to first make a short list. The list will have seven items. Though any pre-chosen number will, of course, serve equally well, let's agree on seven throughout, if only because it's a prime number and so will not easily settle itself into neatly opposing pairs.

---

✍

### The Light List

Giving yourself no more than two minutes, list now, in no particular order of importance, the seven best qualities about yourself that come to mind.

1.
2.
3.
4.
5.
6.
7.

---

Now take these seven items and write them out in the form of a sentence or sentences in which a person with those qualities is described in the third person. For example: if your items were agreeable, good sense of humour, good cook, reliable, self-sufficient, creative and entertaining, your paragraph might read something like:

> He's an agreeable sort of fellow, good sense of humour, a good cook, reliable, self-sufficient, creative and entertaining.

Now, imagine what might happen if we were to add the words 'in public, but ...' He's an agreeable sort of fellow, good sense of humour, a good cook, reliable, self-sufficient, creative and entertaining in public, but ...

But what? What do 'buts' like this in conversation warn us of? Exactly: contradiction, the lurking presence of opposites. Because of this implication of the words 'in public, but ...' we now expect to hear that this person described is altogether different in private. And so we might easily construct a Private Shadow that is something like:

> ... but in private he's completely disagreeable, devoid of humour, eats like a pig, is unreliable, dependent on others to the point of despair, fettered by logic and inaction and bores himself silly.

Of course it's not always true that all seven of the items on the Light List, the Daylight or Outdoor List, will have direct opposites in the Dark or Shadow or Private List, but it is astonishing how familiar appear some of the characters created by single or multiple pairs made up from the respective lists. (We'll be looking at variations on this game later in the Fiction section where we explore developing characters in stories.) For instance: the woman who is the life and soul of the party but who is wretched at home; the self-proclaimed Great Self-Sufficient One who cannot go for more than a minute without the attention of others; the man who says he's going to w̄ the Great Novel one day but spends all his time convincing himself he's not ready to start yet or, even more common, spends all his days in the pub talking about it until it seems as if there's no mystery left for him to uncover.

In any of these pairs we can find the raw material of a realistic 'fictional' character, drawn between two polar extremes. But it is only when we tackle all the pairs as aspects of the *one* character that we really begin to get an insight into what makes this character tick. And of course the characters we are talking about here are ourselves.

Let's say there's this guy who likes to think about life and health and action, and every now and then he is actually quite active, but most of the time, mornings especially, he lounges around in bed or, when he does manage to get up, finds numerous excuses for not getting down to what he really wants to do: write a book.

A single pair of items taken from my own Dark and Light lists might give me the preceding paragraph as the basis for a short story. In many ways, in fact, it has much in common with the structure of fairy tales. Though it doesn't quite begin with Once Upon a Time, it does begin by describing a situation of stasis, a situation where nothing much is happening. Though in fairy tales the stasis tends to be of the pleasant variety – Once Upon a Time there were three little pigs who lived with their mother in a lovely little house where they were all warm and happy – there is no reason why the stasis cannot be of a less enjoyable kind, as in my scenario above.

But if there is stasis, the next immediate requirement is change. 'And then,' say the fairy tales, 'one day ...' And everything changes. (While we're at this point, it should be noted, of course, that it is also possible to start the story at the point where the change takes place. 'Jeremy Hoddle lost his job at the zoo.' However, it is likely that the next few sentences will give us a flashback to the good – or bad – times of Jeremy's recent past. Otherwise, of course, there would be no sense of forward motion in the story.)

ow a story or a fairy tale works, how does it
lifficulties or problems when we sit down to
a start, if we were to spend some time every
ooking at our own shadows, we might begin to
ich we could integrate (to use a Jungian term)
the shadow and so be able to draw on its considerable ener-
gies. If, for example, we are always writing happy stories and
find we are going nowhere, might it not be a good idea to try
to incorporate some of the Shadow tensions within ourselves,
if only to help us feel connected and involved in our own
writing.

Someone said that all writing is autobiography, which it
may well be, and if this is so it may well follow that writing
that is not capturing our full attentions is writing that we are
not fully involved with. The Shadow game allows us to see
aspects of ourselves, for a moment, in the third person and so
gives us an opportunity to see how our own story might connect to whatever writing we are engaged with.

## NO. 3 – THE CRITIC

*'Unless you think you can do better than Tolstoy,*
*we don't need you'* – James Michener

The third Inner Figure, who is related to the Shadow but who,
because of his/her strength, ought to be treated as a wholly
separate entity, is the Inner Critic. For some of us, this critic is
a supportive player, helping us when we get stuck and
suggesting ways out of problems we might have. For a lot of
us, however, this critic just sits there, doing and saying nothing, until we try to do something for ourselves and then he or
she starts muttering somewhere in the back of our minds
about how all this is a joke and how someone like us can
never be a writer because (a) we never went to university, (b)
we went to university and it destroyed our creative abilities,
(c) we must be joking if we think we can be as good or better

than so-and-so, etc. Every one of us has to battle against these voices and try to find a space and a way to write against the odds, and this is whether or not we ever go on to try to publish, a whole new ball-game in itself.

In some senses, this inner conflict is the most difficult thing about writing in anything other than just the occasional fits and starts that have probably brought many of us to this book. If I write only occasionally, I can convince myself that the reason I don't write more, the reason I don't practise more, is that I couldn't be bothered or that I don't really feel there's any point to it. If I write regularly, on the other hand, it becomes harder and harder to deny the feeling that there's a part of me that thinks I'm not good enough or maybe even that I'm too good and the world simply doesn't understand my genius. And it's not really true that this is just a cop-out, though that's how it might seem. It's more a case of an inner conflict between the part of me that wants to write and the part that thinks I'm not really up to it. Getting these two parts to start communicating with each other would certainly help the writing process for most of us, and even though these peace talks are something that may continue all our writing lives, there are a couple of ways by which we might get the dialogue started.

As with any breakdown in communications, the first thing to establish is a relationship between the two partners through a third intermediary. All this is not terribly far removed from the process going on in Northern Ireland where two sides spent a long time refusing to speak to each other, or the situation that occurred between the USA and the USSR during the Cold War. 'You Russians eat your children.' 'You Americans are only interested in money.' What is needed is an intermediary third party.

In our situation, left to our own devices in the privacy of our minds, we have to invent a third party to chair the negotiations between our Inner Critic and our Writer. This third party is an objective referee who sympathises with both sides equally but has no investment in either. The desire of this third party is simply to establish dialogue. For us this third party is a piece of paper and a pen, or a typewriter or a word processor, and, as with many of these exercises up to now, a strictly enforced time limit.

Let's imagine the northern peace talks again. Two sides refuse to speak directly to each other. What happens? A third party is called in to chair sessions in which each of the original parties (and not necessarily even in the same room) air their opinions and differences and then the thrust of these is passed on to the other for its response. In the same way, we need to allow our Inner Critic time to air his/her views, no matter how much we might dislike hearing them or seeing them written down in the cold light of day. Because only by getting these views, all of them in all their negativity, down before us can we really start to come to grips with their reasons for being and so come to understand and deal with them.

## The Critic Speaks

Let's say we take our piece of paper or word processor, write on the top of the page 'The Critic Speaks' and then, for just five minutes, or five whole agonising minutes, blast away at ourselves and all the reasons why we'll never make writers of any sort. We might start out something like this.

> You want to know the reason why you'll never make a real writer? Well, for a start, you know damn all about it. You never really studied English, except in school and even there you never really paid attention. And since you left school you've hardly read more than a few dozen books and most of them you didn't even take in and couldn't remember anything about them if you were asked. The only reason you want to be a writer is that you have this stupid notion that writers are somehow above other people and that poets in particular are some kind of sacred laity.

But it's all bullshit! You don't even read other people's poetry yet you go around saying how much poetry means to you. What you actually mean is how much YOUR OWN poetry means to you, and that's the whole problem with you and writing: all you want is an audience for your feelings because you don't want the world to forget you when you pass through it like the little forgettable flea you are.

Now if your inner critic comes up with something like that, and, believe me, most of us will have to face criticism from ourselves that is a lot worse, then you've got to resist answering with something like Ralph Waldo Emerson's snappy: 'Taking to pieces is the trade of those who cannot construct.' Sure, you can get into a bawling match, but it won't get you anywhere. A wiser next step might be to put away the paper or switch off the word processor and leave things lie for a while. The most important part of any negotiation of this sort is calmness and, faced with that kind of lacerating critique of ourselves and our desires, it's only natural that we should immediately want to retaliate with even more wounding words, which would get us nowhere. When the Critic airs his or her opinions like this, it should be remembered that the Critic is frustrated and ignored by us most of the time (except maybe when we're feeling sorry for ourselves), and so all of this hostility is pent-up and may well be exaggerated. By giving ourselves a bit of breathing space away from the subject for a while, when we come back to read over what the Critic has said we will often find that we can recognise at least a small bit of truth in what he has said. If we can concentrate on this small bit of truth and concede this much to our Critic, then it might be possible in turn for him to concede that he has exaggerated various aspects of his complaints against us. For instance, isn't it true that, despite our interest in writing, we really don't read as much as we know we should to keep abreast of what is happening? And isn't it true that somewhere, maybe deep down, we do feel that our education, university or otherwise, is incomplete and that we have missed opportunities along the way for improvement? Whatever they are, there are undoubtedly points in the Critic's raving with which we might be able to agree if we could only be sure that he wasn't going to suddenly jump on us again and hammer us into the floor.

But now this can't happen. The Critic has joined in the debate and the debate has a chair, an intermediary. The Critic has put his complaints down on paper and now he must allow you to offer your defence in a similar fashion. So you write down what you feel is your defence, trying to allow yourself to concede to the Critic those points where you feel he is not wholly wrong, and at the same time possibly suggesting reasons why the situation with your writing is as it is.

## The Writer Responds to the Critic

Yes, it's true that once in a while I feel I may not have the learning and education I might wish for but, when it comes to writing, imagination and courage are also a large part of what is required, and I am sure that if I could find the strength to commit to writing on a regular basis this extra knowledge could also be picked up along the way or learned. I'm not saying that I will ever write the great Irish novel or whatever, though it would be great if somehow I was able to give it my best shot. All I'm saying is that by admitting defeat before I begin, all I can look forward to is defeat. The fact is there is no one kind of person, or no one kind of education, that results in a writer. History and the world around us now is full of writers of all sorts who have triumphed over adversity, disability, censorship, indifference or direct hostility, and it is as full of writers who are waiters, bankers, diplomats, housewives and unemployed as it is of people who are full-time professionals or teachers of English or Literature or Creative Writing in education establishments. It is commitment and talent that make good writers, and whatever talent I might have I will only discover with commitment. And if you are right in the end and I do prove to be no good, or no great good, in the process of trying I will find out something about myself, I will find out something about writing and I will learn to appreciate more the writing that I admire because I will have seen both the difficulties and the joys that went into the making of it. All I'm asking is that you give me a little time.

And then you make a deal.

Let's say, every morning for twenty minutes for the next ten weeks, I sit down and write. That's all, just to get a routine going. Will you agree that for those twenty minutes you'll sit back and say nothing and give me the chance to see what I can really do when I'm allowed to believe I might just be able to do *something?* What I plan to do is take on the exercises and games in this book, one after the other, as if they were designed especially for me to tackle, and then, at the end of that period, both of us will sit down together and look through my rough drafts and if we see *anything* that looks interesting or promising then we'll make another agreement for another period of time.

To convince the critic, you might then add:

And so that you won't feel left out of the process, because you obviously have your own strong ideas on what is and isn't good writing, when we get to the end of that first period, or even once a week if you like, you can go through the work and give me your suggestions as to what could be improved. And if you come to something you don't think can be improved, no matter what I do, something that is just complete rubbish, in your opinion, we'll agree to leave that aside as it is. We'll agree that that was just necessary for warming up in the way a musician allows herself the occasional bum note when trying to work out a new tune or melody.

These letters from the Critic, and back to the Critic in response, are obviously just rough examples, but you get the idea. We're not terribly interested in how good you are at writing letters just now, and we also don't want to smooth over too quickly the very real conflicts that are likely going on inside you if you're like any writer I've ever met, but the whole process of formalising, of ritualising, if you like, this communication between 'the writer you' and 'the inner critic you' can be one of the most rewarding and perspective-changing activities you can take on. It can too, with luck, patience and perseverance, lead to a whole new approach to writing, conferring on what was once a difficult and stomach-churning process the gift of discovery.

## NO. 4 – THE GUIDE

Now we've looked at the Poet (Novelist, Artist), the Shadow, who is that part of ourselves which we do not always acknowledge or maybe even cannot see or bring ourselves to see, and the Inner Critic whose insights, were we able to harness them, might well help to add edge to our writing. And we might be coming to the conclusion that all Inner Figures are obstacles for our writing, forces which are working against us getting anywhere. But there are other Inner Figures who, were we to make contact with them, would be only too willing to help us in our efforts to put meaningful words on paper. Primary among these is the Guide, a figure who, as her name suggests, exists to help us but who, like all guides, must first be approached for help.

Imagine you're alone on the planet trying to write. You're alone there in the room where you write, but even when you go out and sit in a coffee shop or walk up the street or take the bus, you're still alone. You know as a writer that you're supposed to be tuned in to things and people around you in the world, but the more you tune in the more you realise you're *outside* the world looking in, or locked *inside* your head looking out, and the more alone this makes you feel.

The truth is, however, that all of the above is at worst a lie, at best an illusion. For just as the language you use when you write – the vocabulary, syntax, connotations and denotations – have been inherited by you after being passed on by others, so too, even when you seem to be all alone writing, you are actually connected to a line that goes all the way back into so-called pre-history. The fact is that no writer is ever truly in isolation, no matter how bandied-about that term might be. Just as every time you speak you are responding to all the speech you have ever heard, when you write you are responding to all the things you've read and to all the ideas you've had about reading and writing. If we were to ask ourselves, for instance, what was the most important book we've ever read, in terms of changing our opinions or our perspectives on the world, what might the answer be? The Bible? Well, that is certainly one of the most read and (half) known books around, and it's likely to be one that influences many of us at some level of our being. But what else? What was the first book that really made you want to write? It may not, of course, have been a great book. It may have been *Biggles* or the *Famous Five* when you were a child, or it may have been your first encounter with Serious Literature. Or it may not have been a book, inside covers, at all. It may have been a story or yarn you were told once and you felt it would be great to be able to tell a story like that. What I'm getting at here is that our influences, literary and otherwise, are many and varied, and often it is a hugely liberating and energising thing to re-make that connection with one of your basic influences.

Put it like this: say you were offered the chance to bring back to life any writer from history, published or otherwise, so that you could hear his/her story. Who would you pick? Some people immediately say Dickens or Shakespeare or the anonymous authors of the Bible or Gilgamesh or whatever, and some of them will mean it. For others these names will be more or less dutiful responses to the question, when what they would really like, what they would really enjoy (to use a word that doesn't come up terribly often in creative writing handbooks) is to bring back to life the great-grandfather who wrote that four-line note your mother has always kept in her secret hiding hole of family treasures. Or the author of the newspaper clipping about the wedding of your mother and father. Or the author of the first scribbles in the first jotter you had in primary school which is, you're sure, still under a bed or in a cupboard somewhere. The point is, when we strip off the attitudes that we have assumed gradually along the way to wanting to be a writer, we may find that there are all sorts of real impulses, real questions and real relationships that we have ignored and which, if explored, could lead to real writing. The young John Montague seems to have discovered something very similar:

'At the back of an extremely boring class one day, I was scribbling and suddenly the words came alive. It was an equivalent of one's first discovery of sex, a profound mental and psychic thrill. And I knew I was hooked.

## The Guide Exercise

Let's try the game. First of all, on a sheet of paper, write down, as an un-numbered list and in no particular order – just as they occur to you – the names of 50 people who have ever lived and who have had some influence on your wanting to write or on what you have written so far. Remember, it is very likely that this list will contain not just writers but friends, acquaintances, historical figures who may never have written anything but whose lives or deeds have, in some way, spurred you on to write. Negative influences as well as positive: the teacher in school who laughed at your work; the publisher who rejected your first stories; Hitler or Stalin who persecuted artists and writers and who helped you realise that challenging accepted 'truths' was your calling too. Taken like this, it could be anybody, quite literally.

But, of course, there will be writers there too. Not necessarily literary figures (my own list might include Carl Jung as well as great and lesser writers like WB Yeats and Richard Brautigan), the people on your list will have added something to the written inheritance of the culture. And your favourite writers may be there too, as may the writer whose book you are reading at the moment. What book *are* you reading at the moment? What novel, what guide book, what cook book? That person qualifies for consideration for your list, and if you don't think this is true then why are you wasting your time on that book when there are so many that could better repay your attention that will go unread?

So write down the list of 50. For this exercise you don't really have to charge headlong as you have done in earlier exercises. You'll find you need to think a bit about this one. At the same time, don't allow yourself to slow down so much that the task of coming up with 50 names seems too daunting. When you feel a 'sequence' of names coming up – maybe you're thinking of the names of teachers, or of pop stars whose song lyrics once reverberated in your head – go with the sequence. You can always shorten the list afterwards (a little bit of editing is *always* a good idea), and it certainly helps to focus the mind to have to make decisions about exclusion. If, on the other hand, you find it impossible to come up with so many names, maybe it would help to draw up a preliminary list of fields of endeavour (i.e. novelists, poets, singers, painters, doctors, relatives, whatever) and then try to write a subordinate list to each. Finally, when all of the categories are completed you could try to edit down the total number to 50. (As in all of these games, it is necessary to have a final goal. Otherwise the thing would just never get done. Ask the thousands of people who are constantly telling you about the book they're planning to write!) Remember that on another occasion you may come up with a slightly or even radically different 50 people, so by doing this exercise you are establishing nothing for all time. You are simply examining what you perceive as your influences in this one moment. OK, do it now and then we'll go on with the next part.

Assuming you've done that, here's some part of what might be my own list:

CARL JUNG

FLANN O'BRIEN – maker of nonsense of Pythagorean proportions

RICHARD BRAUTIGAN – American novelist and poet of disturbed, sentimental and achingly beautiful writings

DENISE LEVERTOV – American poet of total engagement

EMILY DICKINSON – the first woman poet I ever heard of! Brevity, simplicity, hallucinatory images

PASCHAL SHEERAN – a school friend who read Dostoevsky and whom I looked up to for that reason

When I look at this list, even on reading back over this page a couple of days after originally writing it, there are things I want to change. That is not *really* what I think or want to say about Flann O'Brien, or that is not exactly what I feel about Denise Levertov. But that's OK. I change, and my feelings and my impressions change from minute to minute, second to year. If I sit here and wait for the definitive list, or the definitive anything, I'll be waiting a long time. So let's move on.

> ✍
>
> Now you've got your list of 50 names in front of you. It took a while longer than you might have expected, and there are things you would like to change and people you would like to substitute, but that can wait for another time. If you thought the first bit was difficult, now you've got something else to do: now you've got to further edit down that list of 50 to a list of 10. You've got to go back through those influences and pick out the 10 that hold the most power, resonance, respect or affection. Give yourself 10 minutes to do this, then come back to the third part.

Now you've got a list of 10 people, and this 10, probably, will be the 10 that most often crop up when you play this game, with the occasional substitution. In fact, what I am proposing for the final part of this game might very usefully be carried out with each of the people from this new list, one after the other over a period of weeks or months.

*

What I want you now to do is select one person from your list of ten, the one person who, on consideration, has influenced you in one way or another to want to be a writer or to write. I'm trying to keep this definition as open as possible so that you don't now opt for someone you're happy to be associated with and will gladly acknowledge. It would be far better to pick that name who, despite everything, is still the one, deep-down influence. The point is to select the one name from the list who, if you were a diviner, would make the two rods tremble when you passed over it. No one can tell you who this person is: only you know. Take your time and then select your person.

The person you selected becomes your Guide, your Special Correspondent, your Ideal Reader, your Mentor. The person you selected becomes your Muse, your Visitor, your Breath, your Inspiration, whatever name you like to use. The game you have been playing is actually a very significant ritual of belonging and inheritance. At some level, by choosing the people you did, all the way from 50 to 10 to 1, you have chosen a single person to be your Guide. Indeed, there are some who would say that this person has chosen *you* to be guided. When you think about it, mythologies and fables are full of people being guided and guiding, and isn't there always the feeling, even when it's not stated, that the guide was waiting for the supplicant to arrive, just as the supplicant has always been looking for that guide?

So too with writing. Just as we often feel we are all on our own in the task of trying to make sense of the world, so too has someone gone before us who has felt and dealt with the same feelings and who, if only they could be here with us now, would help us through and spur us on to new heights. If only we could combine our meagre but unique talents with the giant talents and untutored passions that have come before us.

But maybe that's exactly what we can and have to do. Maybe that's what writing is all about, making that primal connection. Carl Jung would have seen it as tapping into the Collective Unconscious, while others will see it as the inheritance passed down through a family or a throne, or the genetic code passed down through the line. It doesn't matter how we think of it. What's important is that we do think of it and we do explore it as a prelude and companion to our other creative writing.

## Getting to Know Your Guide

Now that we at least have a name, we're going to look at ways through which we might get on more intimate terms with our Guide.

1. Start, as we started in the Inner Critic game, by writing a letter to your Guide. What do you want from him or her? What do you *need* to know? Obviously if we could bring Dickens or Shakespeare or Sappho back from the grave there are any number of questions we might like to ask, but we don't want to demand too much of the Guide in case she turns away from us. The Guide will have more respect and time for us if we first think about what we want to ask, if we come to her with a clear idea of how we would like her to help. So what do you want from your Guide? Write your question in the form of a letter and maybe include in that letter, as if you were writing to a real person, some greeting, some remarks on how you feel about that person, some indication of the place of respect in which you hold her.

2. Then, write the Guide's response. Dear Pat, Carl Jung will write, thank you for your letter, etc. And he will go on, maybe for just a few lines, to deal with the thrust of my letter or maybe to tell me that I had better think again about what I'm asking. He might suggest to me that I read his own works again (which I know I should do if I am trying to establish a proper communication with him – after all his books are his letters to the world!)

3. If you find that the letters seem to be a little forced in the beginning, this may be because the venture is a new one for you and makes you feel a little self-conscious. To try to free up the correspondence, it might be useful to imagine an event or series of events in which you and your Guide figure have some sort of adventure together. (There is nothing like an adventure to bring two people into some sort of bonded relationship.)

Here's an example, a small part of a prose sequence of my own called *Letters to the Dead*, which describes a number of my own adventures with, among others, Carl Jung.

> Dear Carl Jung,
>
> I had a vision or a dream or one of those memories of something that may never have actually happened. In it you and I were walking along by the side of a river, talking about this and that. Mostly you were doing the talking, but I was more than happy to listen. For a change. You had the air of a friend more than of a teacher. We stopped by the river when I thought I saw something. Sure enough, there was something glinting in the water. I waded in and drew it out. It was a rope, made of golden strands.
>
> You took the rope, looked at it for no more than a second, then threw it back. Then you reached out a hand and helped me back up the river bank.
>
> 'Sometimes they are even made of gold,' you said, 'but still they hold us back.'

If you have done these exercises, and you may of course do them a number of times or do variations on them, you will have built up some form of dialogue between you and this person, your new Guide. The idea then is that when you have completed a first draft of a new work, you 'hand it over to the Guide' to give you his/her opinion on it. When you write as the Guide in this kind of situation, remember to write as fast as you can, without deliberation. Then leave the piece alone before coming back to it to try to make sense of it. If, as I suspect, most of us deep down know our own weaknesses as writers, and know when we are fooling ourselves, a kindly and respected figure like the Guide is probably the best person to throw some light on these weaknesses and to offer us suggestions for improvement.

# OTHER GAMES IN BRIEF

Finally, here are some suggestions for a number of other games we do not have space to explore in detail in this section. There are many other games in the other sections. Experiment with the ones that appeal to you, but also consider looking at the ones which seem *of least interest*. If we are to go looking for surprise, we should go to those places where it is most likely to stand out, where it is least expected.

### 1. Where You Are
Describe, briefly, where you are: the room, the country, the point in your life you have arrived at. How did you come to be there? What are you looking for?

### 2. Be Invisible
Imagine you are invisible. Go outside and look at the world as one who is invisible in it. What do you feel like? What do you miss?

### 3. Questions
Make a list of contentious or impossible-to-answer questions. Who killed JFK? Is the universe finite or infinite? What did my father say to my mother when he was courting her? Write the answers as if you had proof and conviction.

### 4. Letters
As well as writing letters to the dead (as you may have done in your Inner Figures games) write letters to the living. Tell Bill Clinton what you think of his behaviour with Monica Lewinsky. Tell the Pope what you think about the ordination of women. You don't have to send the letters (though you may). The point is to work up a head of steam.

### 5. Manual
Write the opening paragraphs of a manual on some technical subject, preferably one in which you have no great

technical knowledge. How do nuclear generators work? What is inside a computer? Imagine you are trying to explain to a child. Use metaphor, use narrative, use myth.

## 6. Dreams

Keep a notebook of your dreams. If you don't remember them, start remembering them. If you try but really can't remember them, do one of three things: try harder (keep a notebook by your bed); try interrupting your sleep at the end of sleep cycles (sleep cycles last about an hour and a half – if you fall asleep at twelve, set your clock for half past one, three o'clock, half past four, six, half past seven, etc.); make them up (spend a few extra minutes in bed in the morning – it's OK, it's work! – and *pretend* you're having a dream).

## 7. The Triggering Town

*The Triggering Town* is the name of a small book of lectures and essays on poetry and writing by the American poet and teacher Richard Hugo. In the title essay Hugo describes a technique for effectively building a parallel world out of the details of the world around you. Pay great attention to the things you can see, but the things you can't see, make them up: let your imagination link things that are linked for no one else. 'Your hometown often provides so many knowns ... that the imagination cannot free itself to seek the unknowns,' Hugo writes. The next time you go to a town or place which you don't know but which intrigues you, watch things carefully and invent your own explanations, imagine your own sequences of cause and effect. 'It is important that a poet not question his or her assumptions,' Hugo writes in the same book, 'at least not in the middle of composition. Finish the poem first, then worry, if you have to, about being right or sane.'

# *Poetry*

*'At a critical moment, a seafarer tosses a sealed bottle into the ocean waves, containing his name and a message detailing his fate. Wandering along the dunes many years later, I happen upon it in the sand. I read the message, note the date, the last will and testament of one who has passed on. I have the right to do so. I have not opened someone else's mail. The message in the bottle was addressed to its finder. I found it. That means I have become its secret addressee'* – Osip Mandelstam

BEFORE WE START OFF THE POETRY, or verse, or writing-in-lines or whatever you want to call it, section, it seems important to clarify the mission here. There always has been and always will be strong debate on whether writing workshops, particularly poetry ones, can teach people anything. How can you teach someone to write poems of all things? Fiction, maybe, but not poetry. Poetry is something that is felt. And feelings cannot be taught.

As the great Russian poet Osip Mandelstam knew better than most, poems are messages in bottles that we cast out to sea, not knowing where they will end up or who will read them. Probably for this very reason, and more than any other form of writing, poems seem like personal messages, from one particular human being to another. What did Robert Graves say? 'Poets don't have an "audience". They're talking to a single person all the time.' In fact, for many people poems, or attempted poems, are so personal that there can be no way to discuss them, examine them, respond to them and certainly not to improve them. The very idea that there might be ways of *teaching* people how to write them seems ridiculous.

But poems, it is obvious, are also made with words and language, and if there are things about words and language which we must learn before we can communicate adequately, could there not be things about the relationship between words and language and poems which we might also learn?

The answer is, of course, that it is not poetry but the writing of verse and the exploration of mood that is being taught and encouraged, just as it is not song but singing that is taught at a college of music. 'Poetry is emotion put into measure,' said Thomas Hardy. 'The emotion must come by nature, but the measure can be acquired by art.' In a sense, you must bring the poetry with you and the workshop helps you to find a way to deal with it. If you come without it, you're very unlikely to be taught how to make it, but at worst you might just have a better appreciation of it the next time you stumble into it. Not everyone who takes piano lessons ends up in a concert hall, mercifully.

So, you can't teach people to write poetry, but you can coax, provoke, stimulate, encourage and challenge people who have some interest in writing to at least pursue it long enough and with enough dedication to discover whether or not they have whatever it is that it takes. Vague enough?

The poet and novelist Philip Casey, who no longer conducts workshops, though he has done so in the past, insists on this distinction between poetry and verse.

> 'Needless to say, if the writer is a gifted poet to begin with, problems can be solved by an experienced tutor, and this is perhaps the essence of a workshop. However, poetry is so rare and I'm not at all confident that I've written any myself, and therefore couldn't possibly teach how to "do" it. That one can learn "how to do it" is a common misconception and it terrifies me.

I would be much happier if they were called "verse workshops". The techniques of writing verse can be taught with a fair degree of confidence, or at least the problems of writing verse can be solved. Someone who has a good grounding in the techniques of verse is theoretically more likely to write a real poem, provided s/he has the guts to go through their dark night of the soul.'

Eavan Boland, one of the popularisers of the writing workshop among the present generation of Irish writers, and one of its most committed and thorough exponents, sees the workshop as an opportunity for sharing, and certainly not sharing in some kind of vague New Age sense.

'A workshop is a community of craft. The most common problem for writers coming into a workshop for the first time – not just young, but also new writers – is the difficulty they have in taking advantage of this. People progress in workshops by learning to avail of the short-circuit which is there for the taking: of the critical process, of the identification of mannerism, of the very valuable and often generous conversation on offer in a workshop about the writer and the writing.'

The poetry writing workshop, then, is a place where learning and experience of poem-making is exchanged. Like all centres of learning, it might also be said to be a ritual space in which to experiment, to try out new things and as often as possible to make mistakes and to learn with others and from others how to deal with those mistakes. Eavan Boland quotes Chesterton.

> 'Chesterton's remark is a good one for workshops:
> "If a thing's worth doing, it's worth doing badly".
> The soundest advice for workshop writers is to
> bring in their worst work not their best, seize the
> help they get, and – most important of all – raise
> their tolerance level for their own failures.'

Accepting not just the possibility, but also the *probability* of this
kind of failure in advance is a very liberating and enriching
experience. It can also be an inspiring one. If a mediocre
flautist were given the opportunity to play before his peers,
and even maybe before one or two exceptional flautists, the
experience might be a terrifying one, but one which the
mediocre flautist would likely learn from. Even the experience
of standing before an audience which is listening with the
same kind of attention as got the author writing in the first
place can be a very affecting one. And, as Dermot Bolger says:

> 'New writers also need to beware of the views of
> relatives and close friends, who normally cannot
> be objective about the work. Their own
> knowledge of the author and his or her personal
> life always gets in the way of the words on the
> page. You need to find a neutral person whose
> opinion you can trust.'

But when it comes to poetry/verse workshops, as opposed to
fiction or non-fiction workshops, one other ingredient tends to
be present: baggage. Many people come to workshops with
very determined ideas about what poems are, and nothing that
does not fit this mould will do. Other people think that everything is poetry, as if they were rebelling against all notions of
not just 'good' and 'bad', but also effectiveness and ineffective-
ness. Deny these distinctions and you deny difference itself.

Because of all this baggage ('poems must rhyme', 'poems
should never rhyme' etc.) aspiring poets very often have little
idea of what poetry in our time is like. Some poets bring

poems by other writers into their workshops. The US-based Irish poet Eamonn Wall says:

> 'I find that many beginning writers have had little contact with contemporary poetry and really don't realise what possibilities poetry offers them. They want to write poetry that is contemporary in shape, feel, and sound but don't quite know what it is. To help them understand the possibilities, I bring in some poets' work – everyone from Richard Wilbur to Rita Ann Higgins – and we go on from there. It's important at the start to show young poets what's out there, what they can do.'

So the three ingredients of any poetry workshop might be example, challenge and plenty of room to fail. In a sense then every workshop is a game where people play towards a common goal. (And let's not forget that Shelley's masterful 'Ozymandias' was written as part of a sonnet-writing 'game' between himself, Keats and Leigh Hunt.)

If the earlier games in the book were intended just to get us writing and thinking, and in that sense might be called expansive games, this next game takes some elements we've already come across (such as automatic writing) from the expansive group, but uses them to focus, edit and compress. In other words, the earlier games produced the raw material, but this next game will work first towards producing the raw material and then towards editing it down.

## BATS IN THE BELFRY

Before we begin this single most important game in this section, you'll need a watch or clock, as well as the obligatory pen and paper (chisel and lump of stone, if it makes you feel better), because often there's nothing like a good deadline to help get things done. The game is in three parts, but I should say that it's important to play it one part at a time and to resist the temptation to read on to see where the game might be going. Although the game can be played many times – and hopefully you'll come back to it often – for this first outing, at least, travel blindly in the hope that you'll discover something worthwhile on the way. The whole objective here, especially with this first part, is to get yourself well and truly and, for once, intentionally lost.

## Part 1: Getting Out of Your Head

Imagine you're drunk, or stoned, or slightly, or even very, unhinged. (If you're fortunate, or unfortunate, enough never to have had any of these experiences, imagine you're a method actor working yourself up to playing the storm scene in *King Lear*). Take your pen and piece of paper and, limiting yourself to exactly five minutes (hence the watch), rave. Don't worry about the spelling, punctuation and certainly, for the moment at least, not about the meaning. As Nuala Ní Dhomhnaill says: 'Poetry springs from a level below meaning; it is a molecular thing, a pattern of sound and image.' The objective here is to go beyond meaning, to orbit it, to run in tandem to it, in parallel with it, to tap into a kind of sub- or supra-meaningful flow of words and images and to let them out onto the page unchecked. The most important thing here is DON'T LOOK BACK, DON'T THINK and DON'T STOP. (Remember what happened to Lot's wife.) If you stop, even if you don't quite become a pillar of salt, you're likely to feel either stupid or clever, delighted with yourself or worried about what to write next. Either way you will be interfering with the process. Again, the objective is just to fill the sheet of paper before you with words. That's right, quantity rather than quality is what you're after. Ideally these words will form phrases (after all this is a game for producing the raw materials for further work). Therefore it might be helpful to be as visual and objective as possible, to imagine that you're commenting on something that only you can see, recounting a bizarre dream, maybe, or having a prophetic vision. In order not to stop and become self-conscious, it might be a good idea to insert the words 'and', 'if', 'but', 'when' or whatever when you feel a particular picture or phrase starting to run out on you, if only to keep the flow going. Think of yourself as a child who has just come running into the kitchen having seen something strange or wonderful outside and breathlessly trying to recount it, without stopping to wonder what it is or to consider the conventions of punctuation or spelling. Confining yourself to writing in the present tense may also be a good idea as it may help you to make the pictures and images you call up more vivid. And steering clear of the words 'I' or 'me', at least early on, will help to keep you concentrated on external matters rather than on your reactions to them.

If you don't think you need to read back over the first part to make sure you've got it, and if you're happy enough that your wrist can hold out while you're scribbling furiously and non-stop for exactly five minutes, off you go.

## Part 2: The Glistening Bits

You should now have in front of you something like the following – perhaps very different in subject matter, but probably a long, apparently meaningless ramble of a thing:

> Seven bakers in a field running around in circles wearing tennis racquets on their feet and crunching down the ears of corn and singing 'Ave Maria' while a lone crow circles overhead and a dog with a face like Winston Churchill stands behind a camera on a tripod waiting for the perfect moment to shoot etc.

Meaningless, bizarre, unconnected to the real reasons you want to write and certainly not poetry. OK, but full of possibilities all the same, full of striking, strange, particular and maybe even attractive images. Remember, the point was to just get something down, to surprise yourself, to excite yourself.

Now that you've located some of the raw material of the unconscious, the next step is to go back over it and, without worrying too much at this stage about where it's coming from or what it's really about – remember we're not going into analysis here – to simply select five phrases from it, of no more than five words each, which for one reason or another strike you as interesting. These are 'the glistening bits'. The reasons that particular things strike particular people may be very involved, but here it might be a good idea to go after those phrases which seem unlike your own voice, phrases which are so different from your normal conversation that they seem stupid, irrelevant, odd or whatever. It might help, too, if they are phrases which engage at least one of the senses. In other words, what you are looking for is TS Eliot's 'objective correlative', those descriptions of things that seem to have the ability to tell us also something about the person who observes them. (As a short aside, consider for a moment two people walking together down the street, one of them in a wonderful new relationship, the other depressed and restless. Even though they walk down the same street and see, more or less, the same things, these things strike them in different ways. Perhaps the happy person is drawn to the colours of the street signs, the occasional flower or even weed managing to push its way up through the pavement slabs, while the depressed person sees only the greyness of the old stone, the rubbish accumulating in the litter bins, the exhaust fumes belching from cars. Without having to tell us he's the happy one or the sad one, if either of these individuals was to write about what he saw on his way down the street, it would give us a pretty good idea of how he was feeling.)

Anyway, to get back to the game, in the above example of automatic writing (which is here not because it shows any great literary merit, but simply because it will serve as an example), I might be drawn to the following phrases:

> Seven bakers in a field
> tennis racquets on their feet
> crunching down the ears
> a lone crow circles
> the perfect moment to shoot

In the third example, 'crunching down the ears', I confess I would have preferred to keep the whole phrase, 'crunching down the ears of corn', but that would have broken my rule of no more than five words per phrase. Though the maximum number of five was arrived at quite arbitrarily, both for the number of phrases and for the number of words making up each individual phrase, until I get to the end of the game my own rule is to observe the initial limitations. Writing from the unconscious, without the imposition of some sort of limit, may take up the rest of your life and produce very little that speaks to your conscious mind. The real trick is to get the conscious and the unconscious (or the left and right sides of the brain, as some people see it) on speaking terms, without indulging either at the other's expense. Clearly, I trust, it is as dangerous to live wholly in the unconscious as it is to live wholly in the conscious.

OK, so now you've got the five phrases in front of you. The next step is to try to connect them, to write the words around them which you feel would bring them together suffi-ciently to make a unit out of them. At this point I should say that you now owe nothing to the original piece of automatic writing (as the pianist owes nothing to the jam session which produces an idea for a new melody to work on). In trying to make connections between your five phrases, you are com-pletely free to change the order of their appearance, even to use one of them as the title of the piece you are working on – though, again for the purposes of this game, you should not give in to the temptation to alter any of the phrases in themselves, by dropping an existing word, for instance, or by inserting a new word which you would like to have been there. The purpose of this rule of the game is to force you to try to find ways to accommodate the phrases intact before giving up and hacking away at them until they resemble the kind of writing you would have produced anyway without the game.

With the only other restriction being the amount of lines you can fit on a single page, now try to bring your five phrases into a single unit without worrying too much about, or forcing, the meaning.

### Part 3: Eavesdropping on Yourself

For many people relatively new to writing, the temptation to 'explain away' the weirdness of the original phrases in the work of Part 2 is almost over-powering. But, as Seamus Heaney has said, 'It is no denigration of a poem to say that it resists its audience for a while.' In other words, some kind of mystery may be what makes poems what they are. And we might add here that the same resistance is often experienced by the author before she/he has had time to live with the implications and inferences of a particular piece of work. Poems that seem to surrender themselves to a single interpretation on first reading rarely have what it takes to bring the author – let alone another reader – back to them again and again, surely the real test of a poem's worth.

Anyway, now you have something in front of you that is composed of lines of words, parts of which you like, parts you don't, perhaps. Perhaps it includes rhyme, or half rhyme, perhaps not. Perhaps there is a general underlying rhythmical or sound pattern, even a sense of metrical unity. (Impossible, of course, to discover either without first hearing the piece aloud.) Either way the objective at this stage is to try to hear the piece, to hear what is going on in it. And the best way to do this is, of course, to read it aloud. Read it yourself, or get someone to read it to you, or read it into a tape recorder and play it back. (A great trick is to play it back on a machine with a variable speed setting, at just above or below your own talking speed, so that your voice seems to belong to someone else.) In reading it, it might help too to walk around with it, to declaim it sometimes, in the manner of a Shakespearean actor, to whisper it at other times as if it were something for possession of which you might be executed on the spot. The idea here is to try to hear the words in a new way, to hear them as a communication from somewhere, and someone, else. Once you've done this for a while, you can safely move on to the final part of the game.

## Part 4: Rewriting

*'Writing is about re-writing, re-writing and re-writing. It's about running through the wall, the pain barrier when the words turn to muck in your mouth. It's about having the humility to recognise the flaws and start again, plus the arrogance to say I have something to say and I am going to say it'*
– Dermot Bolger

*'The best writing is rewriting'* – EB White

The words 'rewriting' and 'revision' send shivers down the spines of many would-be writers, poets especially. Perhaps because of the notion that real poems come to people whole, there has built up a widespread belief that to tamper with the given words of a first draft is to court disaster, and perhaps this is sometimes the case. Certainly if we are to believe the accounts of some of the biggest names in English literature, poems do on occasion come fully formed and it is the poet's job simply to try to write them down. (Coleridge's *Kubla Khan* is perhaps the most famous example of a poem coming ready-made, and the man from Porlock at his door one of the greatest, if unwitting, enemies of poetry.) But before we decide that that's the end of the matter, first we must ask ourselves the old question again about how we learned all the things we know, from cooking to driving to walking. And the answer is that, in the main, we learned by experiment, by interaction, by manipulation. We added more spices or we moved a lever we'd never moved before, and the results were different, and we learned something by encountering that difference. In the same fashion, assuming that not everything we have ever written has come out fully formed and satisfied us even after years in a bottom drawer or some old notebook, the practice of rewriting will at least give us some insight into how words work together and how we work with them. And very possibly it will give us a whole new perspective on the possibilities of all that half-finished work that clutters our ledgers and minds. (Irish poets once had to endure up to seven years of study and training – including physical training to do with breathing and speech – before they could join the poets' guild. And Horace's advice, 'Let your literary compositions be kept from the public eye for nine years at least,' reminds us that even with our acceptance to the guild our work is far from over and we can't expect success. Vladimir Nabokov was typically pointed: 'Only ambitious nonentities and hearty mediocrities exhibit their rough drafts. It is like passing around samples of one's sputum.')

The rewriting section of the game, if we are ready for it now, has two parts: the first consists of drawing up a good map of the terrain so that we don't get completely lost if we happen to go up a siding or want to see what's around the corner ahead; the second consists of driving bravely on.

To make a good working map of a place, for the purpose of finding your way back, you need only register the significant landmarks: where the road turns, the castle on the hillside, the wreck of a car in the ditch or, if there are many cars, the colour and model of the significant one. With these essentials you can be almost sure to find your way and find your way back again. Similarly, to make a working map of a poem, the things you really need to register are not necessarily the subject matter and the why-I-wrote-this-in-the-first-place stuff, but, more than anything else, the nouns and the verbs. It is mostly through the nouns and the verbs that the poem does its work.

The notion that poems have levels, some 'deeper' than others, has always bothered me, implying as it does that in reading a poem we're in a kind of lift shaft where going down is somehow better than going up towards the surface, the 'deeper' level somehow better than the clear view from the rooftop. Instead I like the notion that the poem has many parallel worlds to it, alongside the more obvious narrative world, the what the poem is 'about', if you like. And the poet's job in rewriting or revising is to explore these parallel worlds and see how they might contribute to the over-all effect.

One way to access these parallel worlds is to go back through the poem, noun by noun and verb by verb, and consider what way the poem might have turned if some change had been made at one of these pivotal points. A poem, for instance, that has the word 'field' in it, meaning a defined space in the countryside, might easily lead off into other kinds of fields: fields of vision, fields of study, battlefields etc. Similarly a poem that has for one of its lines 'the man grasped the thistle' might easily have used that word 'grasp' as a doorway into the notion of seizing knowledge, as when the same man grasps the solution to something. By going back through the poem like this, sensitive to the*connotations* as well as the *denotations* of the words, a poet begins to have some idea of what the poem is really 'about', of just how expansive (or not) the language truly is.

## ADJECTIVAL INFESTATION

There is a second advantage to this kind of responsive examination. Subjected to this level of scrutiny, weak nouns and verbs are quickly exposed, and often a poet will see that a string of adjectives called on to puff up the importance of a noun ('the long, thick, metal bar between the wheels') means that the noun itself should probably be changed to something more exact ('the axle'). Similarly nouns that too readily suggest standard adjectives ('rolling seas', 'piercing blue eyes' etc.) should be parted from their mass-produced accessories. If an adjective seems to belong perfectly to a noun, it's likely the wrong one. Adjectives must be earned. If in doubt, go with Mark Twain's (witty, pithy, precise, earned, slightly caustic and yet undoubtedly reasoned and therefore simply good) advice: 'When you catch an adjective, kill it.'

The second part of the rewriting section of the game is one where instinct, time, energy and commitment really come into play. Some poets say it takes them dozens of rewrites to get a poem to the point where it is finished (or abandoned, if you agree with Robert Frost). Others say their best poems happen in the fewest rewrites, coming out almost full-born. In this matter there can be no 'hard and fast' rules. But there seems to be plenty of evidence that the poets who engage most fully in all aspects of their writing are the ones who are graced most often by complete or semi-complete poems. In a very real sense, they make their own luck.

The choice of whether to make rhymed or unrhymed, metrical or free verse poems lies ultimately with the poet, and these matters are covered in more detail elsewhere in this section. While some subjects and moods seem to demand a particular approach and formal response, there can be no doubt that to a great extent these questions are answered (or not answered) at an unconscious level. It seems likely, however, that a poet who has no experience of anything other than formal verse will be unlikely to produce many free verse poems with which she is content.

In my own experience of writing, and in co-ordinating writing workshops, I can only say that, now more than ever, I am convinced of the truth of Norman Mailer's assertion that 'In writing you have to be married to your unconscious. You choose a time and say, "I'll meet you there tomorrow."' And it seems to work. You make a date, and make sure to turn up yourself, and it happens. As in any relationship, the unconscious, or inspiration, or whatever you like to call it, can only be expected to open itself up to you once it has established your commitment and intent.

In school almost twenty years ago, I had a teacher who was particularly fond of the expression 'bats in the belfry'. He used it when he wanted to single out a particular student for humiliation. 'Mister X has bats in the belfry,' he would say, meaning Mister X had difficulty keeping track of what was going on in the classroom because of his inability to control other ideas whirring and screeching around in his head. I'm not convinced that that particular teacher added in any way to my love of literature or my understanding of the human condition, but that expression has always stayed with me, seeming effortlessly to describe something which terms like 'the unconscious' or left-brain/right-brain theories do not quite get.

Bats in the belfry announce their presence in a number of ways: thin noises in the dark, occasional sightings at the windows or under street lamps, droppings to be swept up by the sacristan. Some people spend their whole lives going to church (or not, as the case may be) with their heads covered in case the bats should swoop down and get tangled up in their hair. Once safely inside, they believe they are the only living creatures in the building. Poets, on the other hand, or anyone deserving of the title, see everywhere traces of the invisible lives with which they share the world and know it is as likely that those invisible lives are contained within them as without.

## ALTERNATIVE APPROACHES

OK, that previous game, which was really a series of games tacked on one to another, was intended to show how one might move from the general automatic writing game (from Section One) into something focused a little more on a goal, i.e. something poem-shaped. For instance, when we see a piece of text on a page broken into lines which do not quite reach the margins of the page, we know, or at least expect, that it is a poem. Poems, for many of us, have a particular look or sound.

But there are whole traditions and movements and histories of poetry which have produced things which do not look or sound like that at all. For example many people raised in our era will believe that poems differ from pieces of prose in that they have rhyme, or metre, or assonance, or alliteration, or any of a large number of features which have helped to define poetry of previous eras. But the truth is that none of these things are essential to poetry, or, more correctly, that the presence of none of these things will ensure the existence of a poem.

Earlier I mentioned the distinction which the poet Philip Casey draws between poetry workshops and verse workshops, and it might be said that the features I have been talking about in the previous paragraph are features of verse (which may include poetry) rather than features of poetry itself. Now, rather than get lost in a discussion on what poetry itself actually is (at best we could guess at what poetry up to now has been like, but poetry is always reinventing itself), it might be more useful to look at a form which seems to have little physical or surface relation to what many of us regard as poetry and, having explored this other form, to then see if there are any grounds for similarity between these two quite opposite traditions.

The tradition I am talking about is the haiku tradition, one in which I claim no expertise but introduce now partly to break the western tradition's dominance, under which so many of us labour, and partly because the concentrated form of the haiku seems an ideal training ground for any verse (or poetry) writer. And, so often, training is what seems to be missing. As poet Fred Johnston says: 'There is an apprenticeship to poetry as there is to most decent things. But nowadays this apprenticeship is passed over in favour of the ready-made, the immediate.'

# HAIKU

A haiku is a short poem, of Japanese origin, comprising a total of three lines (though this is flexible), the first of five syllables in length, the second of seven, and the third again of five. Actually, one can find many haiku which have neither three lines nor anything like 17 syllables (variants on, and interpretations of, the haiku form) but for our purposes we will stick for the moment to this more rigid formulation.

> *On the cardboard box*
> *holding the frozen wino*
> *Fragile: Do not crush*
>    – Nicholas A Virgilio

Haiku, also called hokku, was originally the opening section of a longer form of poem, the renga, which originated in thirteenth or fourteenth century Japan. About the beginning of the nineteenth century, haiku began to appear in France and in the following decades was introduced to the United States where it was popularised by writers such as Ezra Pound and later by a generation of poets like Gary Snyder and Robert Bly. The so-called Beat Generation of writers was very much influenced by the haiku and related forms and by the philosophies that seemed to come with those forms: compression, simplicity, etc. (Among contemporary Irish poets, this kind of compression is perhaps most notable in the work of Dermot Healy.)

For the western writer, the attraction of the haiku as an exercise is obvious. The writer is faced with the challenge of trying to compress his or her essential details into a very compact form, but in attempting this, and in abandoning ideas of rhyme and metre as seems inevitable (though see Paul Muldoon's rhymed haiku sequence *Hopewell Haiku*), he or she can often discover a kind of pure poetry in the form's simplicity. The movement called Imagism was strongly connected to the haiku and related forms because it stressed the importance of the image itself over the way in which that image might be 'narrated'.

It is interesting too to observe that the haiku in its traditional form also includes a *kigo*, that is a word or phrase which suggests the season or time of its composition. The fact that the original haiku poets were often nature mystics has a lot to do with this, but it is also a useful way to remind ourselves to focus on physical details without being allowed to directly name the season. (In all of the written arts, the dictum, as we're probably fed up hearing, is 'show, don't tell'.) The 'secret' – if one wishes to take on the traditional challenge of haiku – is to include the *kigo* without sacrificing the poem's integrity. Hence Nicholas A Virgilio's subtle use of the word 'frozen' in the example quoted above.

Other poets have taken the basic haiku form and allowed themselves to vary the numbers of syllables or lines, or both, while keeping to the idea of the haiku as a moment, an awareness, a fleeting glimpse of something. Among a number of poets who have successfully written linked sequences of haiku is Irish poet Michael Hartnett (1941–99) whose *Inchicore Haiku* beautifully and movingly records moods and feelings seldom found in haiku:

> *What do bishops take*
> *when the price of bread goes up?*
> *A vow of silence.*

And writers interested in the effects of haiku, and syllabics in general, will be certain to read the work of poets such as Paul Muldoon and Marianne Moore, both of whom, in very different ways, push against the edges of form and challenge expectation even while their poems are celebrations of pattern and the pattern-making instinct itself.

This idea of a pre-set form into which poets must place their syllables only after painstaking counting and weighing often seems foreign and 'a million miles from what poems are about' to western readers. But, when we think about it, the natural ballad and sonnet forms in which many of us effortlessly produce 'verse' are equally predetermined: the sonnet must be 14 lines long, have a particular rhyme and stanza scheme etc., but it is also a refined syllabic unit, each standard line of iambic pentameter having, as we will see, 10 syllables. The integration of another culture's poetic system, far from obscuring the workings of our own, for many poets helps to bring the essence of that system into view.

Let's take a very short look at the opening of one of Marianne Moore's poems, 'The Steeple Jack', which in total comprises 13 stanzas of 6 lines each. To some eyes and ears this arrangement may seem arbitrary and perhaps it is. I confess I don't know. In fact, a sense of the arbitrary, a sense of chance playing a role, is part of the experience of reading almost any of her poems. And at the same time the poems are built, measured and built. The first stanza or verse of 'The Steeple Jack' reads:

> Dürer would have seen a reason for living
>   in a town like this, with eight stranded whales
>     to look at; with the sweet sea air coming into your house
> on a fine day, for water etched
>   with waves as formal as the scales
> on a fish.

It seems to have no shape (though 'whales' and 'scales' at the ends of those equally indented lines do rhyme). But then if one reads on something interesting happens. The 'arbitrariness' of the first stanza seems to be echoed in the succeeding stanzas, until the reader realises that there is a correspondence in form between stanzas. And not just a correspondence, but almost a perfect mirroring. If we were to count the syllables of the lines of the first stanza, we would come out with 11/10/14/8/8/3. This might well be someone's phone number for all I know, but if we go on to count syllables in the second stanza we find the pattern is exactly the same 11/10/14 ... Moore has settled on a form which may be arbitrary or accidental, but she has taken that form as seriously as someone who spends hours at a rhyming dictionary hoping to complete the perfect heroic couplet.

To get a sense of how haiku works (or how haiku work – the word haiku is both plural and singular) the best way to go is to start to write them. Because of space limitations, it should be pretty easy automatically to lose much of the baggage we bring to writing poems as speakers of English (rhetoric, hyperbole, repetition) and concentrate on the all-important images. As space is so limited, only the essential ingredients of an event or description can earn their place. The wide blue sky will probably have to become the blue sky which will probably have to become the sky which is anyway a more inclusive image. Haiku succeed in being inclusive because of their brevity, while loquacious western-form poems, by giving themselves the licence of duration, may tend towards exclusivity.

We might say that the aim of art is to pass on the emotion or insight gained through a particular experience to enrich the whole of humankind with individual experience. However, to recreate that experience for somebody else, we need to not simply *tell* what the emotion was, to render it second-hand, but to also *remake* the world as it was, and the forces in it, at the time of the experience in the hope that the experience can be relived imaginatively and thus shared by the reader or listener. To understand this is also to understand the need for control and editing and selection in writing, for if we did not control or edit or select we could only in vain try to reproduce all our lives up to the moment of the experience – obviously a futile act. To make art, then, is to select as much as it is to respond or create. To make the comparison between a child and a childlike artist, we might say that one of the essential differences is the presence of a refined selective process in the childlike artist's experience-informed working. When it comes to a form which might help in developing processes of editing and refinement, simplification and distillation, it is hard to find anything to compare to haiku.

The first thing we need to find is an image. This can be a bit like thinking about symbol (which we'll look at later on), in that often to see either you have to momentarily look the other way. Images, like symbols, are forms of connection, and it's hard to see the connection between things when you're looking directly at them. And the image is unlikely to be framed by an 'I', a narrator, as is common in western poems, because we simply don't have time or space for all of that. Where a western poem will say 'I wandered lonely as a cloud/ That floats on high o'er vales and hills,' haiku will say something like 'Clouds over the valley. Golden daffodils.' No 'I', no lonely; nothing of the narrator but his representations of the world through which we must decipher his feelings, his insights. Simple though it be in construction, the haiku's simplicity is what gives our western minds most difficulty. Which is why occasional attempts to write them are probably good for us.

> Keep a journal in which, every day, you write at least three haiku on whatever topics or subjects come to mind. Don't worry if you have no ideas. Write down 'No ideas' and then try to make that into a haiku-shape. What we need to do is get used to this foreign form.

Here's one, just thrown together.

> *No ideas. Spring*
> *outside the window all day*
> *and no sign of growth.*

That 'and' is a bit of a waste in a third line which might have more inevitability and resolution and a bit less 'staging' and 'delivery', but you can see the idea. For one thing, the form is adhered to. And, for a second thing, one of the original concepts of haiku is kept: that the images find their home in the natural world and that the poem, despite an unpromising and conceptual beginning, does find its way back to the world pretty smartly.

But a great many haiku come from a moment of observation. And in many ways haiku are the verbal equivalents of those Zen paintings for which the artist might have sat for hours or days or months in contemplation, though the finished painting was produced in a few flicks of the hand.

> *Lovers in the park.*
> *Her hands holding his hands down.*
> *Gift of powerlessness.*

My western mind likes all those h's in that second line (because I cannot deny my inheritance, maybe, or because I feel they hold the line down, sound-wise and visually, almost like those pins you tack a wire down with), though my haiku spirit warns that powerlessness is a very conceptual word on which to end a poem that should find its power in being 'earthed'. A further consideration is the number of syllables in that final line, actually six, though some people pronounce 'power' as if it were a single syllable. So neither of the two minds or mind sets is completely happy, but both are allowed access to a new process, and new processes are what we must continually bring to writing.

For those interested, I should point out that there is another member of the haiku family which is quite popular. The tanka, as it is called, is like a haiku with a two-line extension: its five lines have 5/7/5/7/7 syllables respectively. Other variations exist but it might be more interesting to develop your own, like Marianne Moore.

Finally, before you get on with experimenting with your own, a word on images in haiku. The haiku, like any poem which derives energy from the juxtaposition of images, will often in the first two lines place together two images that at first seem unrelated and will then, in the third line, draw these images together. Often as not, these images will come from some kind of polar-opposite bases: if the first image is of a detail like a flower (a microcosmic detail), the second image will often be of something like a star (a macrocosmic detail). Similarly if the first image is of the outside world, the second image will often be interior. Without pushing this idea too far, awareness of this possibility of bringing together polar opposites, dark and light, yin and yang, good and bad etc., in haiku is one of the form's great attractions.

With enough theory for now, go ahead and compose some haiku. If you think you occasionally need a change of form, either break the convention of 5/7/5 or, better still for our purposes, like Marianne Moore, invent and then stick to your own.

## SOMETHING IN PARTICULAR

One of the things haiku is very good at drawing our attention to is the power of the particular over the general. In fact, all creative writing relies on the potency of the particular to make comments on or conduct examination of the general. Whether we like to think of this as the relationship of the microcosm to the macrocosm or of the concrete to the conceptual, one of the main points about creative writing is that we are always trying to find the image which will concentrate our attentions. It is for this reason that we would do well to consider the business of strangeness here before we move on to the next section of the book.

In an article on the attractions of strangeness, in the March/April 1998 issue of *Poets & Writers* magazine, David Long wrote:

> 'The less you read, the likelier you are to fall back
> on commonplace truths, or half-truths, and the
> ordinary schmaltzy way of expressing them. But
> reading works saturated with strangeness is both
> disturbing and oddly encouraging. As Kafka
> suggested, They're a blow on the head. At the

same time, they offer a mandate. They say:*Look what X managed. You can manage it, too, can't you?* Further, they teach you to recognise strangeness, to acquire a taste for it. Strangeness, you learn, is an antidote to the awful sameness of received ideas. Seeking it becomes a moral imperative.'

What Long is calling strangeness here, many of us might call *The Something in Particular* (to use the title of a book of poems by the Belfast-born poet John Hughes). And whatever fears some may have that the attraction of strangeness might have too much to do with novelty and not enough with lasting worth, we might do well to consider it in our own approaches to writing. For if every life and event and place is made up of hundreds and thousands of possible stories and poems, then we'd surely be crazy to avoid the strange, especially when we know that, by definition, it's an opening into a new realm of seeing. Look at how contemporary American poets like Charles Simic and Jean Valentine, or UK poet Carol Ann Duffy, or the Irish poets Dennis O'Driscoll and Leland Bardwell use an initial strangeness to draw readers into their poems. Here's just a handful of sample opening lines:

### Charles Simic
'*Go inside a stone ...*' ('Stone')
'*Grandmothers who wring the necks / of chickens ...*'
   ('Classic Ballroom Dances')
'*We played war during the war ...*' ('The Big War')

### Jean Valentine
''*Standing there they began to grow skins ...*' ('Pilgrims')
'*The house in the air is rising ...*' ('Autumn Day')

### Carol Ann Duffy

*'Out walking in the fields, Eley found a bullet ...'*
  ('Eley's Bullet')

*'The most unusual thing I ever stole? A Snowman ...'*
  ('Stealing')

### Dennis O'Driscoll

*'That she is a widow.'* ('What She Does Not Know Is')
*'The weight of sadness escaping like a gas ...'* ('Voyager')

### Leland Bardwell

*'If only he would admit to being born ...'* ('Brother')
*'The wind blew West from the sun ...'* ('The Mad Cyclist')

Notice how a good opening line, a little bit like our 'He appeared' game from the first section, not only captures the attention but contains enough mystery, enough strangeness, to make us want to keep reading. And this strangeness need not necessarily be a question of subject matter (every story need not start with someone turning into an insect, as Kafka's famous *Metamorphosis* does). It can be, and indeed often is, a question of the manner in which the story or poem is enacted. (Whose is the voice of the poem? What kind of mood is the voice in?) If we shy away from the strange we only rehash all that has gone before us in the book called What Poetry Has Been. Without the strange, and the opportunities it provides, we might as well accept that Samuel Johnson's famous put-down was intended for us. 'Your manuscript is both good and original,' Johnson placed the bait; 'but the part that is good is not original, and the part that is original is not good.' As readers and writers alike, we are interested in difference, connection, the particular, the unusual and the strange, all of these being ways to the heart of our mission: the centre of change.

# WORD CHOICE

Speaking of change, but in a different context now: when does a ghost change into a spirit? When does night become the dark? By this I mean if English is as full of synonyms (words of similar meaning) as it is, when and how do we decide to change one word for another, and how do we decide which is best?

Clearly, no two words have *exactly* the same meaning. Even similar words have different resonances, different connotations. Speak them out loud to hear what they mean. You might say, for instance, that a ghost is what you see in a haunted house, a spirit is what leaves a body when it dies, a shadow or shade is the darkness cast by the dead one and a spectre is something cold and distant. You might also say that spectre is a 'thin' word, while ghost, with its 'o' sound, has breath in it, volume; it takes up space. Like the word mist, with which it shares a final sound, ghost dissolves away and thereby suggests something that itself dissolves. Think how different, how irreverent, the word spook is in comparison: different sound, different resonances, different connotations.

An ordinary crossword-solver-type thesaurus will give a listing for ghost something like the following: n. spirit, spectre, apparition, shade. *Roget's Thesaurus*, however (a book with which every writer should be familiar), will at once require you to be more specific about what you want, and at the same time offer you connections you might never have considered. Under its heading for ghost it will offer you words grouped under the subheadings: shade, which includes apparition; fallacy of vision, which includes mirage, phantasm, vision; and apparition, which includes demon, monster, succubus and vampire, the more obviously fleshy range of the market. It is clear that choosing the 'right' word where many are on offer will not only help to describe the experience with respect both to meaning and sound, but will also send ripples of suggestion shooting up and back through the rest of the vocabulary of your poem.

# WESTERN FORMS

For the remainder of this section we will concentrate on one of the aspects of poetry or verse writing that arouses most debate among practitioners and critics alike. If most hand-books on verse spend most of their time discussing metre, rhyme, etc. and then go on to look at alternative approaches such as the haiku and tanka, I have purposely looked first at the haiku in particular and syllabics in general to impress in our minds the idea of image and compression. With that done, we can now look at a system with which, at first at least, we feel ourselves more familiar.

## 'HOMER WROTE IN DACTYLIC HEXAMETER WHILE SHAKESPEARE FAVOURED IAMBIC PENTAMETER'

*or*

## A SHORT INTRODUCTION TO METRE

Does the title of this section frighten you? For a lot of people trying to write poems, this whole business of metre and the strange terms used to describe it is utterly terrifying. Over the next few pages, I'm going to see if we can find a way to demystify this whole subject, or at least the basics of it, once and for all.

So, let's start with the basics: what is it? Metre itself might be described as the system of measuring 'the alternation of accented and unaccented syllables in English' (Frances Stillman, *The Poet's Manual and Rhyming Dictionary*). Accented and unaccented syllables? We might even decide to call these heavy and light syllables, or stressed and unstressed syllables, or x and y syllables, if it helps. All we're saying, so far, is that metre is made up of two parts, which is pretty sim-ple, one x and one y, just like chromosomes. Now where do we go from here? The commonest metres in the English language today come from the Greek and Latin schools and were also among the commonest metres used in the time of Shakespeare. Of these we will look at the four most common, namely the Iamb and Trochee (the two more common of them), and the Anapest and Dactyl (the two less common of them). And for good measure, sorry about the pun, we'll thrown in a quick visit to the spondee and the rather menacingly named amphibrach.

But where other reference books might seek to explain these terms and/or chart their histories back through Latin and Greek, we will be seeking only to establish a general idea of what they are, how they differ and then, most importantly, how they might be explored to produce new material for creative writing. We'll pick up a few technical ideas, I hope, but we'll be concentrating on application. And don't allow yourself to be put off by the names (all Greek to me). Let's just see if, behind the big words, there are clear and relatively simple ideas.

The notion of accented syllables and unaccented syllables is one that often causes difficulty, partly because it's not something we have to think about consciously when writing a letter or speaking a sentence. When I'm working in schools, I often get the students to imagine a drummer with only a snare drum (the one with the wire mesh on the underside which makes that crashing noise) and a hi-hat cymbal (the one which is like a thin plate turned face down over another thin plate and which gives a light, almost hissing sound.) Now, using these as our models, we might say that the variation between accented and unaccented syllables is like the variation we get from hitting first the snare drum and then the hi-hat cymbal, hard/soft, heavy/light, accented/unaccented. If we were to say that metrical lines in verse are made up of combinations of accented and unaccented syllables, we can see how someone commanding even such a simple drum kit could follow our metrical measures.

Take for example this line from Shakespeare's 'Sonnet 64', which most of us will remember from school.

*When I have seen by time's fell hand defaced ...*

Now, agreeing that we will represent accented syllables by reproducing them in bold print (and in capitals) and unaccented syllables in standard print, this is what the line might 'sound' like for our drummer:

When **I** have **SEEN** by **TIME'S** fell **HAND** de**FACED** ...

In other words, the drummer hits hi-hat, then snare, then hi-hat, then snare, etc. Many of us will already recognise in this pattern what is called iambic pentameter:

Di **DUM** di **DUM** di **DUM** di **DUM** di **DUM**

The word iambic here describes the basic two-part pattern of light and heavy (hi-hat and snare), while the word pentameter (think of pentagon, pentagram) simply means there are five of these two-part measures (or feet) to each line. The iamb and its opposite the trochee (heavy, light) might also bring to mind the heartbeat, no doubt part of the reason that the best known iambic pentameter form, the sonnet, is so associated with love and lovers. This connection between the two-syllable measure and the heartbeat is also one of the reasons for the way in which we form our first vocalisations as babies. We want at once to communicate and to feel safe. Here's a snippet from a diary I was writing in 1992, which might illustrate what I mean. I'm in a library in Co. Fermanagh, working with two groups of school children, one from each community.

> Being Writer-in-Residence in a northern place like Enniskillen, especially when you come from a southern place like Portlaoise (best known for its maximum security political prison), is not something I take lightly. I take it so seriously, in fact, that I find myself going right back to the beginning.

'Ga ga,' says one girl (grey uniform), after much encouragement from me, and most of the others laugh.

'Gu gu,' says one boy (grey uniform again) and most of the others laugh again, though one or two are looking at their hands.

'Da da?' I say to a boy in blue, all confrontation.

He looks at me for a bit before answering tentatively, 'Ma ma?'

And this time everybody laughs. Everybody.

We've all gone back now to our first childhood words, back to just after the heart-pumped, iambic/ trochaic womb, and we're all the same again back there, back here. Safe, comforted. Before Armalites, prisons, firebombs, *Top of the Pops.*

In the same way, we might lift the cloak of mystery and technical language that covers the main metres in the English language. After all, almost everything about structure and metrics has some origin in the physical world. If you're not completely sure about the system of differentiating snares from hi-hats, accented syllables from unaccented ones, then maybe you should have a quick look back at those last few paragraphs before you continue. (It's always a help to read the lines aloud; after all, we're talking about a way of measuring and differentiating *sounds.*)

## STRESS MANAGEMENT

Now if we've taken on that idea that syllables come in the stressed (accented) or unstressed (unaccented) variety, the next logical step is to look at how those two elements might be combined. The first way is that they could be thrown in together any old way at all, and more or less that is what happens when we write or speak naturally. Or is that true? Is it true that when we speak naturally accents and 'unaccents' just come in any old order? What about when people ask questions, tell jokes, give directions? Can't you tell, in fact, from the rhythm of a person's speech what kind of mood they're in? Clearly, even in 'ordinary' language, 'stress management' plays a part.

In poetry, then, stress management is likely to be a big player. If a poem is to have the biggest possible impact, to ignore the interplay of stresses is unthinkable. So how do stresses come together? Where do they like to settle in a sentence? Think of a joke. Better still, think of the punch line. 'To get to the other side.' Where are the stresses there? Imagine yourself choking with laughter (unlikely) as you try to deliver the punch line. What words would you find yourself determined to force out. *Get. Other. Side.* Can you hear that? The words *to* and *the* get lost easily, but we can work out, more or less, what you're trying to say. So there's a connection between stress and meaning. The important words and syllables tend to be the stressed ones. We know this instinctively. When we are saying something important, we tend not only to put stress on the most important elements, but also to move them towards those parts of the sentence where stress automatically falls: in particular to the end and beginning. When I start to speak or write a sentence, you have a fair idea of where you are, because of the sense of something new beginning, but if I go on too long, or deviate too much, or just keep adding material that is of no great interest, it becomes very difficult and you get lost, so if I haven't already delivered the news I've just failed. (See what I mean?) The opening and the closing are important. In narratives and drama, there are other important areas (and we'll look at these in the next section), but even in sentences and phrases they exist. If the start and the ending are important, then sentences of just a few words or syllables should feel *very* important. And they do. Compare 'Jesus began, gradually, to feel tears welling up in his eyes,' 'I should like to hand you in my notice' and 'I feel a very strong affection and attraction to you' to 'Jesus wept,' 'I quit' and 'I love you.'

Interestingly, in the three examples above, most of the words have only one syllable (Jesus, a proper name, is the exception). So it might well be that stressed words, when they have only one syllable, are even more effective than words of many syllables, one or more of which is stressed. Going back to the pub where the earlier joke was told, imagine someone laughing and, at the same time, trying to accept the offer of £20. '**AB**so**BLEED**in**LUTE**ly.' It's funny because it plays with the idea of stress and our expectations of it. But lose your temper with the speaker and ask him straight, hard, does he want the money or not, and what he'll say is: 'Yes' or 'Yeah'. One syllable, one stress.

From all of this it's relatively easy see how the management of stresses into regular patterns came to be such a major feature of poems. In fact, some would say that this play with stresses is actually the *origin* of poem-making. Either way, however it happened, different systems of organising and patterning developed, just as they developed in music and painting and architecture and politics and everything else.

The simplest of these patterns had to do with having a certain amount of stresses in each line of a poem, but these stresses could fall more or less anywhere. Alliteration only added to the drive of the lines. Here is a sample from the fourteenth century, from William Langland's *Piers Plowman*.

> *I seigh a toure on a toft trielich ymaked,*
> *A depe dale binethe, a dongeon there-inne*
> *With depe dyches and derke and dredful of sight …*

> *(I saw a tower on a raised place, excellently built,*
> *a deep valley beneath, a dungeon therein*
> *with deep dark ditches, dreadful to look at …)*

If your ear wasn't going to catch the stresses there, all that alliteration certainly sounds the alert (hey, this stuff is catching!). But Langland was writing for listening audiences. He was 100% interested in and dependent on sound. You might say that the invention of printing relieved poets of some of that responsibility (or deprived them of some of those riches, depending on your point of view), but certainly once books began to appear the whole shape and organisation of English poetry changed. According to Ivan Illich and Barry Sanders in their *ABC: The Alphabetization of the Popular Mind*, Chaucer was one of the first English poets to recognise 'the emerging literate mindset of his courtly audience', and his more complex sound and sentence structures confirm this. He wrote in the knowledge that if something was missed it could be returned to, re-read. It is believed Chaucer died the year Gutenberg was born. The invention of movable type revolutionised writing and printing, and therefore poem-making too, as has, to an extent, every major communications invention since.

Which is why the challenge of finding my own voice, a voice from my own time, is the biggest one facing any writer. There is no one vocabulary, no one set of rhythms or patterns or shapes that automatically makes poems. As we've seen, some cultures have concentrated on aspects other than stress (syllabics, etc.) while others have seemed interested in almost nothing else. If we decide to explore and manage stress, we might remind ourselves that even here there are a number of possibilities: random stress, regular numbers of stresses in a line, regularly placed stresses within the line itself. Regularly placed stresses within the line itself is what we are now going to look at. In particular, we're going to look at those patterns and arrangements that dominate English-language writing and have dominated it since before the time of Shakespeare.

## COMMON FEET

Let's look now at some of the different types of feet, or measures, mentioned earlier. As we'll see, these basics of metrics (and I'm reducing this to the absolute basics) take up no more than a couple of pages and can be absorbed in a few hours. Yet so many beginning poets skip over them and then spend the rest of their writing lives wondering if they have missed something crucial.

Though there are many different kinds of metre found in English verse, here we'll stick to the four main ones and then have a quick look at two others that might be of interest. To further simplify the process, we'll look first at the metres that are made up of feet or measures consisting of just two syllables. We've seen the iambic already, but we'll start with that again, just to make sure we're clear on it. As we look at each metre in turn, it might be a good idea to jot down a few lines of your own in the same metre to get the sound clear in your head.

### Iambic

The iamb, from which we take the adjective iambic, is a foot (measure) which contains two syllables, the first of which is unaccented (hi-hat), the second of which is accented (snare).

**Di DUM di DUM di DUM di DUM di DUM**

Hence the measure might be said to be rising, or forward moving, as the succession of light and heavy syllables seems to drive the rhythm strongly forward. Example – the line from Shakespeare quoted earlier or this line from Derek Mahon's 'Day Trip to Donegal':

**We REACHED/the SEA/in EAR/ly AFT/erNOON**

You might have noticed that in that last example from Derek Mahon I've added diagonal lines, or forward slashes, to separate the different measures or feet in the line, but I don't want you to worry about that too much. The lines are simply there to help you see the pattern more clearly and have no other function. Some people will recall from their school or university days that there is also a system of describing accented and unaccented syllables by placing little signs above them, a little dash or accent ( ´ ) to describe accented syllables, little ( ) shapes to denote unaccented syllables. All we're looking for here is an agreed and simple way to denote these differences.

### Trochaic

Like the iamb, the trochee is again a foot containing two syllables, but this time it is the first syllable
which is accented (snare) and the second which is
unaccented (hi-hat). If the iamb seems to be positive and forward-driving, the trochee might be said
to be hesitant or falling, as it starts strong and then
weakens.

**DUM** di/**DUM** di/**DUM** di/**DUM** di.

Example:

**TY**ger/**TY**ger/**BURN**ing/**BRIGHT** ...

(from William Blake's 'The Tyger').

Or, just made up:

**NO**, I/**CAN'T** make/**SENSE** of/**MET**rics!

(In each of the above examples, you can see that there are
only four feet, or measures, per line, and not five as in the
examples given for the iamb, but this is just to remind us that
what we're considering here is the construction of the feet
themselves and not the number of feet to any given line. The
method of describing how many feet there are to a line we'll
leave to the end of this section, when we'll have this business
of metrics relatively clear.)

Two-syllable feet, which we've just looked at, are pretty simple. After all, if they have only two syllables, and each of the
syllables must be either accented or unaccented, heavy or light,
there are only two real possibilities, light/heavy (which we've
seen is called iambic) or heavy/light (which we've seen is called
trochaic). A metre consisting of two accented syllables does
exist (it's called a spondee, hence the adjective spondaic – The
**LONG**/day **WANES**;/the **SLOW**/**MOON CLIMBS**, from Tenny-
son's 'Ulysses') but it is rare and appears only as a variation in
lines of other metres (usually straight iambs, as above). For
our purposes we can just note its existence for the moment
and move on.

Now let's look at feet made up of three syllables.

### Anapestic

An anapest is a foot containing three syllables, the first two of which are unaccented, and the third of which is accented.

Di di **DUM**/di di **DUM**/di di **DUM**

Example:

*There's a **GIRL**/with a **FIST**/full of **FING**/ers*

(from 'Here Come the Drum Majorettes' by James Fenton) though in this example, Fenton has added an extra unstressed syllable at the end. In a sense, the anapest is related to the iamb, in that both start light and then get heavy, though with the anapest the 'build up' takes longer, resulting in a sound that might suggests horses galloping.

This very suggestive sound is one of the reasons anapests have often been used in poems with equestrian subject matter. Presumably it is also one of the reasons it is the predominant metre in Fenton's poem describing, by sound at least as much as meaning, the passing of a parade.

### Dactylic

A dactyl is again a foot of three syllables, and is, in a sense, the mirror image of the anapest. This time it is the first syllable which is accented while the second and third are unaccented.

**DUM** di di/**DUM** di di/**DUM** di di/**DUM** di di ...

Example –

**THIS** is the/**FOR**est pri/**MEV**al,

the/**MUR**muring/**PINES** and the ...

(from Longfellow's *Evangeline*)

If, as we've seen, the anapest could be said to be related to the iamb, the dactyl, starting strong and then falling off, is like an extension of the trochee. For some people, the sound immediately recalls the rhythm of a train, and this might be a good way to remember it. Another useful memory aid might be to note that the word dactyl is Greek for a finger (think of pterodactyl), and in the human finger, the first, or base, joint is longer than the second and third. But just as every language has its own inherent colour and texture, so too does it have metres and rhythms that sound natural to it. If the dactyl is hardly a very common metre in English (except as a variation), it was certainly up to the task of Homer's *Odyssey* and *Iliad*.

As an aside here we might note that the dactyl is also the basic unit of waltz rhythm (**ONE**-two-three, **ONE**-two-three), so that if Homer and Daniel O'Donnell should meet up in the afterlife they might have more in common than we would first expect.

Finally, the last metre we'll look at in this three-syllable section is the terrifying-sounding amphibrach, again a metre that one does not come across very often (at least not comprising whole poems), but one which might usefully be examined for our purposes. The word amphibrach is Greek for 'short at both ends' and that pretty succinctly sums up the measure.

### Amphibrachic

The amphibrach is a foot consisting of again three syllables, the first of which is unaccented (hi-hat), the second of which is accented (snare) and the third of which is again unaccented (hi-hat).

Di **DUM** di/Di **DUM** di/Di **DUM** di/Di **DUM** di

We don't need to worry about this here too much (after all, the sharper of you will already have seen how the above line could equally be read as consisting of first one iambic foot, followed by three anapestic feet, and with one extra unaccented syllable tacked on at the end). If you're totally lost at this stage, don't worry. Just listen to this line from Paula Meehan's 'Home' and then maybe experiment with reproducing the sound.

The **WISE** wo/men **SAY** you/must **LIVE** in/
your **SKIN**, call/it **HOME** …

And there we have them, the main metrical units of English prosody (and a few of the less common ones as well). If you're not sure that you've taken them all in yet, go back over them from time to time and don't just read them but write them too. All that remains now is to clarify what we mean by our title 'Homer wrote in dactylic hexameter while Shakespeare favoured iambic pentameter'.

It's as simple as this. If iambic and dactylic (and trochaic and anapestic and spondaic and amphibrachic) all refer to the construction of the feet or measures used (and we're not frightened by those terms any more, are we?) all we've got to do now is figure out what pentameter, hexameter, trimeter, etc., refer to. And the answer is very simple: the number of feet in the line. If the prefix *penta-* (remember pentagon, penta-gram?) indicates something with five parts, iambic pentameter must simply mean a line with five iambs in it, in other words a line of five iambic feet. Similarly Homer's dactylic hexameter is simply a line composed of six (*hexa-* being the prefix that indi-cates six parts) dactyls. Thus, if we wanted to experiment with writing lines of anapestic pentameter, we need only remember that an anapest is a 'di di**DUM**' foot, and for pentameter we will need five of them in the line:

When the **HORSE**/starts to **BUCK**/you should **KEEP**/
yourself **OUT**/of the **WAY**

Fortunately, because lines of poetry tend not to be much longer than can easily be spoken in a breath (or two), the number of words we need to learn to describe line length is small and, as we've seen with prefixes like *penta-* and *hexa-*, most of them are already familiar from other contexts. In fact, here's probably all you'll ever need to know. Remember, we're talking about the *number of feet* in the line here and not the number of syllables.

*Number of feet*

| | |
|---|---|
| Monometer | One foot in a line. |
| Dimeter | Two feet in a line. |
| Trimeter | Three feet in a line. |
| Tetrameter | Four feet in a line. |
| Pentameter | Five feet in a line. |
| Hexameter | Six feet in a line. |
| Heptameter | Seven feet in a line. |
| Octameter | Eight feet in a line. |

Lines longer than octameter can almost always more usefully be broken up into shorter lines (though see Belfast poet Ciaran Carson's or US poet CK William's experiments and play with even longer lines).

By this stage you can now be confident that when someone says, 'Aha, a line of Trochaic Heptameter!' what is meant is simply that it goes **DUM** di/**DUM** di/**DUM** di/**DUM** di/**DUM** di/**DUM** di/**DUM** di – which is itself quite an unwieldy line, more likely to be broken up into two lines of trochaic tetrameter and trochaic trimeter (four feet and three feet respectively), which, of course, you have figured out already.

To go back again to the dactylic hexameter of our title, from the name you immediately know that each foot will have three syllables, the first of which is accented, the second two being unaccented, and that in all there will be six feet to the line: therefore you could even experiment with writing your own dactyl lines. Let's try pentameter:

> **GIRLS** in their/**BLOOM** can be/**FULL** of the/
> **WONDERS** of/**SUM**mertime

(However, as you can see, strong metre, rather than disguising bad poetry, often only helps to expose it.)

# THE LINE

While we're on the subject of metre we must, of course, say something more about the line. For not only do we need to think in lines if metre is to work, but also we need to realise that line is the basic unit of poetry, regular or irregular. We've mentioned already that line developed out of breath and speech; it is therefore a musical measure. But the line also has other functions: most often it contains a single image or combination of images, so that the poem as a whole has a cumulative effect. The line must also work as a unit of speech so that, even though succeeding lines may play with our expectations of what is to follow, we feel we are on solid ground through the progress of the poem. And within the line itself there are things we should be looking out for: how 'earthed' or 'solid' is this line? Does it have strong nouns and verbs, and are these as close to the end or beginning of the line as possible so as to make it stronger? Again within an individual line we might also try to become aware of the music, the cadence of the language. If the word 'IOU' (meaning I Owe You) is memorable, it is not just because it's clever but also because it appeals to our sense of what makes a pleasing line. It moves from the slender-voiced 'I' sound to the open 'O' sound to the almost breath-emptied 'U' sound. In other words, it forces us to breathe in a certain way, and whatever a poem may or may not have by way of meaning, one of its most potent weapons of persuasion is its ability to make us breathe according to its plan. Line length also gives the poem much of its mood: long lines seem to imply leisure, thought, reflection, while in short lines, just as in short scenes in a movie, we sense action.

# RHYME

If breath, and hence rhythm and metre, are some of the building blocks of a line and therefore a poem, for many people the other great indicator of the presence of poetry is rhyme.

Despite the fact that fashions change and that Homer composed his 27,000 hexameter *Iliad* without the support of rhyme, for many people rhyme is an integral part of the poetry experience. But can we even say what it is? And do we know that there are different kinds of rhyme?

## MASCULINE OR FEMININE?

Most of us recognise a rhyme when we see (or, more correctly, hear) it. Man, can, ran, fan, Dan, etc. These are the simple ones, the ones that most of the textbooks call masculine rhymes. Again, if we really don't like this name we could call them salt rhymes or dog rhymes and then look to see if there are pepper rhymes or cat rhymes to complement them, but the term masculine rhymes seems as good as any other once we shake off any notions we might have of their being 'more important' or 'better' than any other kinds we might discover.

Put simply, masculine rhymes are those rhymes where the final accent of the word (remember our accented syllables earlier) falls on the rhyming syllable. Obviously, one syllable words like man, can, ran, fan, etc., are all masculine rhymes. Two-syllable masculine rhymes also exist: D**VAN**, é**LAN**, etc. because the final accent of the word falls on the rhyming syllable.

Feminine rhymes, in contrast, are those rhymes where the final accented syllable is followed by an unaccented one -**BUR**ly, **CUR**ly, **SUR**ly, etc. Words like **BUR**ly and **BUR**geon, which have similar first syllables but not second, are half rhymes. Other examples of half rhyme, for instance, are cover–shovel; smiling–wildest, etc.

And that, basically, is rhyme. Internal rhyme, as distinct from end-line rhyme, is when a word in the middle of a line rhymes with a word usually at the end of a different line, which seems fairly obvious.

Now the combination of different types of metre and rhyme schemes means that we English-language writers have inherited a number of 'traditional' forms, forms which are almost inseparable from the notion of what poetry is and looks like. Among these are the sonnet, the ballad, the ballade royal, the villanelle, etc., each with its own metrical and rhyme scheme. And while it is beyond the scope of this book to treat each of these in detail, we will take a little time to look at two of the best known forms, in order to make sure that we can put what we have learned earlier into practice.

Let's start then with what is perhaps the best known verse form of them all.

# THE SONNET

Because of the many variations in the rhyming scheme of the sonnet at the hands of some of the greatest poets in the language, the only thing that can be said to define a sonnet is the (almost universally agreed) fact that it has 14 lines. Usually these can be divided up into two sub-sections, the octet having eight lines and the sestet having six. In turn, this first eight-line section is generally seen as being composed of two further sub-sections of four lines each, while the latter six-line section is often thought of as being composed of two sub-sections of three lines apiece or, as with Shakespeare's sonnets, a further section of four lines and then a rhyming couplet (two lines) to conclude.

William Shakespeare was one of the English language's most famous sonnet writers, and for many people the Shakespearean sonnet is the model they identify as*the* sonnet form. This can be best explained by looking at his 'Sonnet 64', which we have already talked about. Because we are dealing here with rhyme (and end-of-line rhyme at that), we are interested only in the last word of each line.

| Line 1 | defaced | A |
| Line 2 | age | B |
| Line 3 | razed | A |
| Line 4 | rage | B |

| Line 5 | gain | C |
| Line 6 | shore | D |
| Line 7 | main | C |
| Line 8 | store | D |
| Line 9 | state | E |
| Line 10 | decay | F |
| Line 11 | ruminate | E |
| Line 12 | away | F |
| Line 13 | choose | G |
| Line 14 | lose | G |

The chart above, in three columns, shows us the line number of the sonnet, the last word in the line and then gives us a way to talk about the rhyming sound used in that last word. What I've done is given each rhyming sound one of the letters of the alphabet so that words that rhyme together are denoted by the same letter. Hence, age and rage are both given the letter B, while choose and lose in the final couplet are both given the letter G. We can say of this sonnet, then, that it rhymes ABABCDCDEFEFGG, the couplet (GG), or last two lines, sealing both the form and the idea of the poem. A Shakespearean sonnet, then, often takes the form of a question-and-answer session in which some conclusion is reached in these last two rhyming lines, or couplet.

But, of course, the Shakespearean sonnet is not the only way to go. There's the Italian or Petrarchan sonnet (named for Francesco Petrarch, the fourteenth century Italian poet who popularised it), with its ABBAABBACDECDE rhyme scheme (the sestet may also be rhymed CDCDCD). Whereas the Shakespearean sonnet permits seven rhyme sounds, the Petrarchan permits only five or four, making it a little more difficult in English, where rhymes are rarer than in Italian. There's also the Miltonic sonnet (after John Milton) in which the break between octet and sestet is less rigidly enforced and may come anywhere in the eighth or ninth lines. Again ABBAABBACDECDE is the preferred rhyme scheme here. Finally, the structure of the Spenserian sonnet (after Edmund

Spenser) testifies to that sixteenth century poet's fascination with interlocking rhyme. Though not widely seen in recent poetry, possibly because of the challenge of its rhyme scheme, Spenser's bequest runs ABABBCBCCDCDEE.

When you experiment with the sonnet form (or indeed any of the other forms described here), remember that the other basic rules of thumb about poetry apply. Try to write in your own voice or a voice in which you are at least interested. Try to make things physical and sensual. Don't let the sonnet form fool you into writing yonder and verily unless you really want to use those archaic words. And remember that you don't necessarily have to end each line with a full stop. In fact, run-on lines, or lines in which a sentence or phrase is continued from one line to another, help to give a poem a feeling of movement, an organic quality that is often lost in repeatedly end-stopped lines. The challenge of making a sonnet at the start of the twenty-first century is a similar challenge to that faced by traditional musicians: to continue a tradition of form, but to keep the tradition alive, vibrant and evolving.

# THE LIMERICK

The other form we'll have a closer look at (if only because its name seems to suggest a connection with Ireland) is the limerick. Actually, we might have looked at this earlier, because its real interest is metrical, but I thought it might give us a break to look at its rhyme scheme before approaching again the cliff face of metrics and scansion (to scan means simply to analyse metre).

Rhyme then, first of all: comprised of five lines, the limerick's rhyme scheme is AABBA. Some writers of limericks, particularly Edward Lear, have allowed themselves simply to repeat the first line as the last, though this seems to defeat too easily the challenge of the form. But, as a popular form, the limerick is perhaps most interesting for the fact that it is composed of more than one main metrical form. In fact, if we look at a sample limerick, we may be surprised to see just how sophisticated it is.

Here's an example hot off the Boran presses and set in Crewe, an inordinately popular location for limericks on account of its many rhyming possibilities.

> *There was a young poet from Crewe*
> *who didn't know quite what to do:*
> *his poems were dull,*
> *so they said up in Hull,*
> *and his last lines neither rhymed nor scanned.*

Now it's easy to see, and hear, that the limerick has two different patterns, not only in rhyme but also in metre. The first and second lines not only rhyme but also have the same metrical pattern, as do the third and fourth lines, and then the fifth line again has the same pattern as the first two. Now, to try to figure out what should have been happening in that last line, we need to understand how the first two lines work.

To get a sense of the metrical pattern, it often helps to read the lines aloud and to exaggerate the differences between accented and unaccented syllables. Hence the first line might be heard as:

There **WAS** a young **PO**et from **CREWE**

which we could describe as, first of all, an iamb, followed by two anapests:

There **WAS**/a young **PO**/et from **CREWE**

Alternatively, if we're really keeping up here, we could recognise that other metre which Paula Meehan made such great use of, the one with the terrifying name, the amphibrach:

There **WAS** a/young **PO**et/from **CREWE**

with the final unaccented syllable chopped off the last amphibrach. If nothing else, this should help us see how different metrical forms may be related, so much so that we can often substitute one for the other. But if this is what is happening in the first two lines (and the amphibrach model does seem to describe the rhythm better than that clumsier iamb-and-two-anapests model), what is going on in the third and fourth lines?

> *his poems were dull,*
> *so they said up in Hull*

This time, we might try, as well as exaggerating the differences, translating them into our beloved dum-di-dum language.

> Di **DUM** di di **DUM**
> Di di **DUM** di di **DUM**

We could then say that the third line was an iamb followed by an anapest (or indeed an amphibrach followed by a shortened amphibrach, or indeed an amphibrach followed by an iamb) and the fourth line was two anapests. However we see it (and probably the easiest way is to describe it as predominantly anapestic with variations), it is interesting to note that what makes this light little form so enduring is likely these metrical variations. And though the limerick is almost always used for light or funny verse (there is something funny about even its sound alone), the lessons we might learn about metrics and rhyme from playing with it could be very useful for our approaches to other, more serious forms. After all, it's impossible to predict what we'll be doing when we stumble onto our next poem. Or, as Michael Longley has so memorably put it: 'If I knew where poems came from, I'd go there.'

# BRIEF NOTES ON TRADITIONAL FORMS

Here are the 'general specifications' of a number of other common or once-common English verse forms. Because of limits of space, we're going to fairly zip through these, but if any of them takes your fancy, or seems impossible enough, maybe take it out for a test drive. The separate sections of poems, by the way, I call 'stanzas' (from the Italian word for a room) in order to distinguish them from verses which, technically speaking, ought to rhyme. Where rhyme is present, I use the form of notation we have already encountered in the handbook, ABBA, etc.

## Couplet
Two-line stanza, often in iambic pentameter and often, as in Shakespeare's concluding lines, rhyming (AA). The couplet, or sequence of couplets, is also a valid form in its own right.

## Tercet
Three-line stanza, the first line of which may rhyme with the last (ABA). Occasionally seen as a poem in its own right. Basis for the villanelle among other forms.

## Quatrain
Very common four-line stanza form and basis for many other forms, including sonnet, ballad, etc. Most often rhymed ABBA or ABAB.

## Ballad
Composed of four-line stanzas, the lines usually in rhyming, iambic tetrameter and iambic trimeter, alternately.

| Line | Metre | Rhyme scheme |
|------|-------|--------------|
| 1. | Four iambs | A |
| 2. | Three iambs | B |
| 3. | Four iambs | A |
| 4. | Three iambs | B |

## Terza Rima

Supposedly invented by Dante, *terza rima* rhymes the first and last lines in (usually iambic pentameter) tercets, and then rhymes the middle line with the first line of the next tercet, and so on. The rhymes are called chain-rhymes.

| Line | Metre | Rhyme scheme |
|------|-------|--------------|
| 1. | Five iambs | A |
| 2. | Five iambs | B |
| 3. | Five iambs | A |
| 4. | Five iambs | B |
| 5. | Five iambs | C |
| 6. | Five iambs | B |

And so on. To complete the form, write a rhyming couplet based on the sound of the middle line in the last tercet. In the case above, you would add.

| Line | Metre | Rhyme scheme |
|------|-------|--------------|
| 7. | Five iambs | C |
| 8. | Five iambs | C |

Because this form is so demanding of rhymes (in eight lines above we've only three different rhyme sounds), it does help to be imaginative.

## Villanelle

A villanelle has five tercets (three-line stanzas) followed by a quatrain. But if *terza rima* seems difficult because of the limitation of rhymes, the villanelle is even more so: the form has

19 lines and only *two* rhyme sounds! Along with this difficulty, the two A rhyme lines in the first stanza (lines one and three, which we'll call A+ and A- for want of anything better) have to be repeated at the end of every tercet, alternating between A+ and A-, and they've also got to form a rhyming couplet at the end of the concluding quatrain. Frightened yet? Probably the most famous examples of the form are Dylan Thomas's 'Do Not Go Gentle into That Good Night' and 'One Art' by Elizabeth Bishop. But we can get a good idea of how it all hangs together from the first three stanzas of Enda Wyley's 'Wedding Gift' (i.m. Raymond Carver, 1938–1988). Remember that the rhyming first and last lines of the first tercet (A+ and A-) appear alternately throughout the poem and also form the final couplet.

> *Salmon leaping eternally against a well-lit sky*
> *bend ecstatic towards the waterfall, in the wedding*
> > *gift you painted.*
> *Like Chekov, I map new routes from the town*
> > *where I'll soon die*

> *but now and then I stop, admiring these fish that try*
> *to tussle free from the river; a push, then they've*
> > *succeeded –*
> *salmon leaping eternally, against a well-lit sky.*

> *If I'd even a year! I make a list: eggs, hot choc, buy*
> *cigarettes labelled 'Now', at last book that*
> > *Antarctica ticket!*
> *Like Chekov, I map new routes from the town*
> > *where I'll soon die ...*

'Succeeded' rhyming with 'ticket'? Again we can see that 'perfect' or 'full' rhymes are not always the only way to tackle the problem of form.

## Sestina

Like the villanelle, the sestina is a very difficult form to master but one which might reward experiment. The sestina is composed of six stanzas of six lines each, and then finishes off with an additional three-line stanza, which, by my calculations, makes it a 39-line form. The good news is that it doesn't rhyme at all. Instead, it keeps itself together and happy by repeating words. In fact, every word which ends a line in the first stanza (and there are six of them) appears at the end of a line in every one of the other five sestets. For the following chart, the letters A, B, C, etc. indicate the actual words at the end of the lines, remember; there are no rhymes.

| | |
|---|---|
| Stanza 1 | A/B/C/D/E/F |
| Stanza 2 | F/A/B/C/D/E |
| Stanza 3 | E/F/A/B/C/D |
| Stanza 4 | D/E/F/A/B/C |
| Stanza 5 | C/D/E/F/A/B |
| Stanza 6 | B/C/D/E/F/A |
| Stanza 7 | A/C/E (with B/D/F internal) |

This cryptic description of stanza 7, I'll have to explain. In the tercet, the last words of each of the three lines are the A, C and E words respectively repeated from the opening stanza. But *inside* each of these last three lines, the remaining three end words must appear. They may appear anywhere, but it is the B word which must appear in the first of them, the D word in the second and the F word in the final line. Who said writing poems was all about dreaming?

# CRAFTY POETS

One small note of caution here: don't forget that form without poetry is only verse, a container (albeit often a pretty one). Advertising executives know this; so too should poets. Lu Chi, the first century Chinese poet, called the poet 'one who traps

Heaven and Earth in the cage of form'. When you explore a form, therefore, look at examples over years, decades, centuries; look at variations from other cultures, other languages if you can. Embrace craft, but don't think it's like taking a part-time course from which you'll graduate in a few months or years. It's an ongoing process. 'For it is not meters, but a meter-making argument that makes a poem – a thought so passionate and alive that like the spirit of a plant or an animal it has an architecture of its own, and adorns nature with a new thing,' as Ralph Waldo Emerson said. Learning the basic structure of the sonnet is not the same thing as writing a sonnet. And free verse is not any easier for all its 'freedoms'. Unless you want to end up with the troubling suspicion that you're really just 'playing tennis with the net down', as Robert Frost described the writing of free verse, you'll want to see how other writers have faced these challenges. And as Irish poet Tony Curtis reminds us, it's all about reading.

> 'Most young poets don't read enough poetry. This,
> of course, is a huge loss to them. It means that
> their first dives into the cold ocean of poetry often
> leave them trashing about or sinking altogether.
> Whereas a little knowledge of the craft and a few
> basic strokes (rhyme, metre, form) might keep the
> head above the waves until their metamorphosis,
> into a minnow with a pen. Poetry: it's all in the
> flow.'

Something must flow, wriggle, even occasionally kick against form. And you may think you 'have' the form but that does not mean you'll 'have' the poem. Form is something you might feel can be learned and therefore known, but poetry is something that is constantly on the move and poems are only snapshots of it in passing. To get to the poem you have to live with the form. Remember what Seamus Heaney said about poems resisting audiences back on page 58? And in the front row of the audience for any poem sits the poet. (In fact, often he or she is the only person in the theatre!)

As for the danger of being spoiled by success, that occasionally happens. If WB Yeats famously celebrated the news that he had been awarded the Nobel Prize for Literature by cooking sausages, others took their celebrations more seriously. The Sicilian tyrant Dionysius II, when not killing people or, in his almost total paranoia, eavesdropping on his slaves for fear they were planning revolt and vengeance, wrote poems. The question of how he managed to balance his two passions could only be answered by Slobodan Milosevic in our own time, but he did. In fact, he almost religiously entered his work in the poetry section of the Olympic Games, but each time he lost. Finally he combined his two talents and threatened the judges. They gave him the prize. True to form, Dionysius celebrated with an enormous party at which he got so carried away by his new-found success that he drank himself to death. Cautionary tales don't come much clearer.

## OLD HAT?

As we can imagine, there are many other traditional and more recent verse forms with which beginning writers might experiment. And there is certainly nothing to stop a writer from inventing his or her own rhyme or stanza schemes if the challenge of working towards form (rather than, say, away from it) seems interesting. But form (in the sense of inherited form, traditional form, classical form) and rhyme are not without their detractors.

On the anti-rhyme side, for instance, there are many who feel that rhyme suggests, as do Shakespeare's famous final couplets, certainty, completion, resolution, before going on to claim that these are qualities which have no place *in our time*, a notion which seems dangerous to me. Certainly, since Shakespeare, since yesterday for that matter, many aspects of the world have changed and continue to change, and the twentieth century in particular saw huge deviations from what was considered intrinsic to many art forms (hence atonalism in music, surrealism and expressionism in art, etc.). And, of course, individual writers must be free, and even encouraged, to make such rules and set such challenges of limitation for themselves. But to make them for a whole culture approaches totalitarianism (which, being an eight-syllable word, is a suitable conclusion to an increasingly hysterical paragraph – but you get the point).

In the end, it's up to you. You're free to write villanelles for the rest of your life, or you can chop up government reports and make verse from your efforts at sticking them back together. If perfect rhyme seems too limiting, experiment with half-rhyme or rhymes that occur only on occasion or only when you want to emphasise certain lines. You choose your own approach when you've had time to consider at least some of the possibilities. To use the title of that Elizabeth Bishop villanelle mentioned earlier, there are many approaches but there is only 'One Art'. It might be wise to observe, though, that language tends to rhyme quite a bit naturally, and, inspiration aside, writing has a lot to do with practice and craft. In short, the poet ought to get to know the properties of her raw material.

## ON 'BAD' LANGUAGE

There is no such thing as bad language. There is only inappropriate language. When someone uses a four-letter word at the family dinner table it is likely to be considered inappropriate, but it is also inappropriate when a politician uses determinedly Latinate or academic language when attempting to comfort the family of a young suicide or when visiting the old in hospital or when praying to his God. Language is about communication (both with oneself and with the world), and good communicators use appropriate language, language which meets their listeners or readers, challenging by times ('Literature thrives on taboos, just as all art thrives on technical difficulties' – Anthony Burgess), at other times clarifying, but always engaging and engaged.

When writers such as Roddy Doyle or James Kelman, or even 'more genteel' poets such as Philip Larkin, use 'bad' language (remember Larkin's famous opening line, 'They fuck you up, your mum and dad') reactions are often predictable: 'the language of the gutter', 'street language', 'the kind of language you'd hear in a brothel' etc. But like all writers before them, both great and less great, these writers are responding to the question of what is and what is not appropriate, what language is right in a given context and what is not. And for them the use of four-letter words of Anglo-Saxon origin (often, interestingly, describing body parts and functions) is appropriate to many situations, and any evasion or censorship of this is wrong. As Walt Whitman said: 'The dirtiest book is the expurgated book.'

In many ways this is the first and most fundamental political question any writer must face. What language do I use in a given situation? The question is political because language is a political tool, as are all tools of communication and commerce. The epigraph to Tony Harrison's famous poem 'V' is a quotation from Arthur Scargill, the organiser of the 1980s miners' strikes in the UK. 'My father still reads the dictionary every day,' says Scargill. 'He says your life depends on your power to master words.' And you can hear that subtle mastery of words at work in Shakespeare's Caesar's famous speech, 'Friends, Romans, countrymen, lend me your ears,' because you know Caesar's equation of friends with both national and geographic identities has a political agenda.

Language is political too because of its history. As the victor in a war is the combatant who, famously, writes the history, so too is he the combatant who chooses the language in which to write it. If in English now we seem to have at least a two-tier system, this is because social and cultural groups identify themselves with and through their use of language. When a country is invaded by foreigners who speak a new language, that new language becomes the language of power, commerce and success, while the old language seems to indicate subservience, old ways and failure.

Even a cursory glance will reveal two dominant threads in the weave of contemporary English. On the one hand, the influence of the Romance languages, going back, as one might imagine, to the Latin of the Roman Empire. The influence of particularly Latin is enormous, having been first the language of the thriving and expanding empire and then the language of a second, even more expansive empire, also based in Rome: the Catholic Church. The spread of Latin is a huge part of the linguistic and social history of Europe. (One must remember that our whole culture of writing and reading, printing and publishing is in a sense a by-product of an advance made in the cause of religion: the spread of the printing press.)

On the other hand, aside from Latin and the Romance Languages that owe so much to it (French, Spanish and Italian), there is that other group on which English is dependent for its variety: the Germanic languages, including those of the Angles and Saxons. To clarify the relationship between the two general groups, in order to appreciate the question of appropriateness or lack of it, one has to go back to the point in history where these two languages first really clashed. That was in 1066 at the Battle of Hastings, for the Battle of Hastings between the newly arrived Normans and the native Britons was really a battle for the supremacy of one language.

When a small force invades a country, to take effective control with only a small contingent of soldiers it first seizes the seats of government and influence, usually including the chairs of ecclesiastical power, but from the outset it also moves to seize control of all major centres of communication. If the printing press, telephone or radio or TV hasn't yet been invented, it at least makes sure that it controls the local assembly and other gathering places and will not fail to post a guard on the equivalent of the High Street, making sure no disgruntled native might be able stand up there and, in his own language, incite rebellion.

And so it was in Britain. Norman French became the language that was spoken in court and in places of power while the native Anglo-Saxon was used only by workers, those obeying rather than controlling centres of power. Norman French became the upper tier, as English did later in Ireland, and in a short time speakers of the native tongue (in this case Anglo-Saxon, in our own case Irish) confined their use of it to themselves, to private occasions. A man looking for a job had best learn to master the new language if he wanted to succeed, and even one who spoke the old language at home must be careful not to use it inappropriately in the new world in which he found himself.

In the long run, a number of very interesting things happened. First of all, the language became two-tiered, in the sense that for many objects, activities and concepts there were now two words, one Norman French and one Anglo-Saxon, co-existing. The famous example is that in English we have one word for the meat of most common animals and another word for each of the animals themselves. For instance, cow refers to the animal while beef refers to its meat, or pig refers to the animal while pork refers to its meat. This is because, for the Normans, the word for pig was *porc*, and it was the Normans who, being in control, contributed to English the language of the table. Down on the farms, meanwhile, pigs stayed pigs. The 'down-to-earth' word was pig; the 'snobs' in the big house called it *porc*. Sheep, said the farmer; mutton, said the king. And a new language grew from the fusion, carrying within it a political history of conquest and colonisation.

The next interesting, and giant, revelation is that, simple as it may seem, it turns out that not only do almost all of these words for the base animals discussed above originate in the Anglo-Saxon tongue, but so too do almost all of the words in those books by Roddy Doyle and others that cause such offence. And this is despite the fact that one can happily use a Latinate synonym, a word which has come down to us through the Roman and Greek languages, without the slightest fear of offence or inappropriateness. Consider a teacher in a secondary school introducing the subject of human reproduction. Does she use the word *intercourse* or the four-letter Anglo-Saxon equivalent, a word popular everywhere these days except in such lectures? The answer is clear: we have inherited, perhaps without consideration, the notion that words of Latinate origin are cleaner and somehow less tainted than words of Anglo-Saxon origin with similar meanings.

The second surprise in this area is what follows from the above discovery. For not only can we no longer simply refuse those words admittance into literature on the grounds of their being offensive (are we trying to pretend we are the Romans, distancing ourselves from our barbarian selves?), but we also have to admit that what we shy away from in them in normal 'polite' conversation (I almost said 'social intercourse') might be the very thing that could commend them to us in our writing. 'The books that the world calls immoral,' said Oscar Wilde, 'are the books that show the world its own shame.'

## SPACE V. EARTH

One of the surprising things about compound Latinate words is just how empty they appear on closer inspection. Transubstantiation, for instance. What does that mean? It means the change from one form into another. But broken down into its constituent parts? *Trans* means across, which is still pretty vague and conceptual; *substance* is what things are made of, not things themselves, which is a bit abstract too; and the concluding *iation* just makes the thing into a noun to give us the impression that it's something we can hold or touch or taste (nouns being the names of things, predominantly), which of course it isn't. In other words, close up, transubstantiation gives us little by way of physical reality, little to touch. Looked at closely, it's still an *idea*. The word 'change', while it's not a whole lot more physical, is at least brief. It does its work in one syllable. It seems, somehow, closer to earth.

The French poet Stephane Mallarmé wrote a letter to the painter Degas in which he made a by-now famous assertion: 'Poetry is not made with ideas: it is made with things or words that signify things.' This notion serves to remind us that poetry in particular, and all good creative writing, attempts to show us something and not just tell us about it. I can tell you about a trick with a bottle and a pack of cards or I can show you the trick so you can experience it for yourself. Which do you prefer? 'I have written a new symphony,' says Gustav Mahler to a friend. 'Tell me about it,' says the friend. There's something about that last example that is obviously fake.

## 'TITLE FIGHT'

Now we can't approach the end of this section without spending a little time on titles. As if they were doorways, poems (and stories) are entered through their titles. The title creates a sense of expectation of what the poem will be about, and then the poet can either confirm this sense of expectation or take the reader somewhere else entirely. But the title is the point of entry. Even poets who assiduously avoid the use of titles for their poems (e e cummings is a famous example) usually end up having the poems referred to by their first lines, which in effect become their titles. A way around this is to title your poems Untitled 1, Untitled 2 etc, but this gets a bit irritating after a while and, of course, it becomes virtually impossible to remember which poem is which. Shakespeare's sonnets are individually untitled and usually given numbers in printed editions, but most people recall them from their first lines.

But titles have another function. Sometimes even just a title on its own, because of the sense of expectation it creates, is enough to get us writing, and there is a lot to be said for keeping a notebook of titles (of poems you have never written) to give you a kick-start on those days where there is something vague moving about in the back of your head and you need an angle to start. Similarly, the titles of poems or collections by other poets are often a great way to focus your attention. Imagine, for example, writing your own poem or poems called, 'Things I Didn't Know I Loved', after the title of the 1975 collection of poems by Turkish poet Nazim Hikmet written while he was a political prisoner. For myself, titles such as Diane Ackerman's *A Natural History of the Senses* or Jeffrey Skinner's *A Guide to Forgetting* or Polish poet Wislawa Szymborska's *People on a Bridge*, to name but three, are often enough to get me started. But I also keep that notebook just mentioned and am as happy to include in it titles I suspect I will never make anything of (*Granny's Rubber Arms, The Invention of Tractors*, etc.) as titles I am sure will produce work, if I'm lucky, some day: *Why I Lived, I Would Leave You This, Sorrow…*

> ✍
>
> Here's a game to play with titles. Take that poem you're having problems with, chop off the title (if there is one) and stick on a different one, either one from your notebook or even one from some-one else's poem. See what difference it makes to change what the door looks like on the house. The first title that comes into your head may not be the best one.

An alternative, if obviously connected, game is to take one of those waiting titles, or even one of those good lines you can't do anything with, and imagine it as the end, not the begin-ning, of the poem. Then write the poem. If the title is clearly a point of major focus in a poem, so too is the closing line or lines. Simon Armitage says: 'I'm reluctant to begin work on a poem unless I have the title, the first line and the last, or at least a clear idea of what they should contain.' Even if, like me, you still feel endings should be discoveries and not just arrivals, Armitage's faith in last and first lines as centres of power is well earned by his own inventive work.

# OTHER POETRY GAMES IN BRIEF

And, to conclude this section, here are a few more ideas for poetry-related games you might play on your own or in a workshop proper. Other games along similar lines can, of course, be devised. Whatever works for you, whatever gets you writing.

### 1. Postcards
Take a postcard, or a small collection of postcards (a mixture of people, places and objects seems to work best). Now imagine that these postcards are a sort of slide show intended to complement and illustrate your poem. Write the first draft of the poem.

### 2. Objective Voices
Choose an object in the room or wherever you are. Imagine this object has a voice, a history, desires and fears. Write a poem in the object's voice.

### 3. Lost Property Office
Imagine yourself in the Lost Property Office of your own life, where all the things you have ever lost (physical and otherwise) are stored. Stepping in there, describe what you see and feel.

### 4. Answering the Call
Take a quotation from a book of quotations, or take a line or two from a poem by someone else. Respond to it as if it were written specifically for you.

### 5. What You Don't Know
Write down a short list of some things you know nothing about. Make a poem out of one of them.

### 6. Non-Poetry Poems
A version of the previous game, make a list of some subjects you think have nothing to do with

poetry. The list might include hackneyed subjects or it might include subjects you find a little embarrassing. Kick-start a poem with one of these.

## 7. Blind Poetry

'Poetry is what Milton saw when he went blind,' said Don Marquis, and Lewis Carroll said, 'Take care of the senses and the sounds will take care of themselves.' So, sharpen your senses. Imagine you're blind, or deaf. Describe what you might sense at a football match, a concert, the birth of a child, etc. Or, where you are right now, focus one sense, say your sense of smell, and take in the scene. As an example of appealing to the senses, look at the opening stanza of 'To the Woods' by the American poet Ron Houchin:

> *Through the open window,*
> *about four inches above its sill,*
> *I smell the night trees.*
> *The light curtain admits pine needle*
> *must and resin scent still slightly*
> *warm from the sun that leaked*
> *through the narrow vents of limbs.*

## 8. Eavesdropping

Listen closely to what that couple in front of you on the bus is saying, or the man talking to himself in the street. Use someone else's words as the opening of a poem.

## 9. Armchair Travelling

Imagine you've woken up in a foreign country and everything around you is strange. Write about the people and objects around you as if you were seeing them for the first time. (Interested parties might like to look at the early work of Craig Raine and the other so-called Martian poets who took a version of this idea almost to its limits.)

### 10. Favourite Story
Retell your favourite story, but leave yourself out of it. Invent a character to whom it happens and then describe the events as objectively as you can.

### 11. Free Associate
Pick any object and write down a list of all the parts of that object and all the words that object suggests to you. Then try to see what connections, other than the object, there might be between the words in your list. Write a poem that begins with the object but goes on to explore these other connections.

### 12. Wakeful Dreaming
Imagine you're dreaming. Everything is more or less normal, but then something extraordinary happens. What is it?

### 13. Tell Lies
The Estonian word for poet – *luuletaja* – also means 'liar'. Tell some whoppers. Bear in mind Jean Cocteau's: 'The poet is a liar who always speaks the truth.' Lie your way to a truth.

### 14. The Gift
The Irish word *dán* means both a poem and a gift. Make a gift of words to someone in particular.

### 15. Respond
According to Kathleen Raine, 'No woman has ever written an epic poem nor ever will. They have certain minor gifts. The great gift of woman is being a woman.' Respond.

### Now it's up to you ...
Play with the forms, invent your own, chase rhymes, meditate on objects, but just get on with it. 'The way to learn to write poetry is: to write poetry,' says James Fenton. 'So we pass directly from the aspiration to the activity itself.'

# *Fiction*

ONCE UPON A TIME, most of the stories we heard when we were very young began, and then they went on to tell us about some character or characters who one day get into a particular or unusual situation. Kids get lost in woods. Pigs get thrown out of the house. Knights have to set off on quests for damsels or justice. Something happens and what happens tests something in the character or characters: their bravery, their intelligence, their patience, something. In these simple stories we get to follow the central character and watch how he or she acts and reacts in particular situations, which are usually related to the reader or listener in chronological order. As the events succeed each other, we can perceive changes in the behaviour of the central character (let's keep it singular just for the moment). Some changes are for the better, some for the worse. But, after a while, we begin to see a direction. We begin to feel we know where the story is leading the character. But then, very often around two-thirds of the way through the story, something happens. The central character does something stupid, or clever for a change, or reckless (depending on what kind of person he is) and at that point the direction of the story changes again. If she was losing she likely starts to win and vice versa.

While this might be interesting, it's sadly all very general. If we were to try to be more exact about it, what could we say actually makes a story? Well, for a start it will probably need a beginning, middle and end (though not necessarily in that order. A thriller may well start with the end, a murder for example, and then go back to the beginning or the middle to show what led to the murder.) And for every writer who agrees with Anthony Burgess when he said, 'I start at the beginning, go on to the end, then stop,' there's another who sides with Toni Morrison: 'I always know the ending; that's where I start.' An additional difficulty is that, because we're drawn in by the characters, the events, the background and the speed of a story, we forget that there might be something bigger than individual stories from which individual stories borrow their shapes: something called Myth, or Story with a capital S, whatever we might call it. Instead of getting caught up in a debate on what constitutes action or excitement, let's take a short look instead at a particular story, one that we are all very familiar with, and see if we can come to any general conclusions about what elements of writing are present in it, what they do and how we might learn to experiment with them. For those of us interested in the novel form, what follows will also apply. If the short story is, in my opinion, directly linked to the poem (in that it attempts to describe a moment, an awareness of change), the methods of its telling are similar to those used in novels. Where the story must compress, perhaps the novel has a little more elbow room, though Kurt Vonnegut warns: 'A novel has to limit itself to the crew of a ship or a family; it's not a great way to process a huge number of people.' But let's get to the story.

## THE THREE LITTLE PIGS

The story I have in mind is *The Three Little Pigs* (though even with this story some of us will have grown up with slightly or radically altered versions of it), and I choose it now because it's both familiar enough for us to feel comfortable with and clear enough in its form for us to be able to look at it more or less objectively. (The fact that most of us will first have encountered it in childhood should also help to ensure some sort of objectivity.

So, what's it got? What are its constituent parts? Well, three little pigs and a wolf, and the wolf eats two of the little pigs, but the third little pig outsmarts him and ends up eating the wolf. Already, if we were trying to compress this story even further, we could get rid of the first two pigs and just have the third pig who *almost* gets eaten by the wolf *twice* and then, the third time, outsmarts him and ends up eating the wolf. So, boiled down (excuse the pun) to this level, all we really need to tell this story is one pig (the one who changes the pattern of pig behaviour and survives) and one wolf. Every hero, or protagonist, needs his opposite, his anti-hero or antagonist, something to grapple with, something to test himself against, something to overcome.

In a classroom situation, there is generally a teacher and pupils, a wolf and little pigs. When I work with school children, I often spend a few hours playing with the story of the three little pigs, partly to see what realisations the students might come to about what is going on between them and me. By way of illustration, here's another diary fragment from Enniskillen in 1992.

> 'The three little pigs are the three sides of the one little pig and the wolf is the fourth. The dark side.'
>
> We've been listening to my favourite fairy tale, my favourite story. We've gone for turnips to the field, apples to the orchard and to the market for a churn for butter. We've rolled down the hill to our house, forcing the wolf to reveal himself as he really is, waited for him to drop down the chimney and then we've collectively gobbled him up.
>
> Now we're quiet and satisfied. We've seen the enemy, the tiny wolf who all the time has been hiding in the pig's eye, and the tiny pig hiding in the eye of the wolf. We're sitting here and you can hear us breathe.

> Two soldiers in camouflage pass by the window, guns levelled.
>
> We are in the pupils of their eyes, as they are in the pupils of ours.

A protagonist and an antagonist, two opposites (or seeming opposites), so what else do we need? Well, Aristotle, who had a theory about drama that will feature to some extent in this section, suggested that the Plot of the drama (and we'll deal with this in more detail as we go on) involves the central character (protagonist) in two relationships: the first is with the second character (the antagonist) and involves the protagonist performing two (or more) actions that involve that character; but the third main action, which Aristotle calls the climax, though also performed by the protagonist, involves not the antagonist but a third character, and this action somehow changes the relationship between the protagonist and the antagonist.

But hang on: protagonist, antagonist? For fear all this is sounding too complicated, let's just go back for a minute to pigs and wolves. Aristotle suggested we need a third character to change the relationship between the third little pig (protagonist) and the wolf (antagonist) in order to provide our story with a Climax. And, when we look at it, it seems pretty clear. If something crucial had not happened to the third little pig, surely he would have acted just as his brothers/sisters did, building a hopelessly inadequate house to keep the wolf out, sitting back in comfort and, two seconds later, ending up in the wolf's belly. But he didn't do that and he doesn't end up like that. Why? Because something changed him, or changed something in him. He read some book, or he saw some film, or he met some other character who changed him.

So who is the third mystery character in the story of the three little pigs? The pigs' mother who appears briefly at the start to set them off on their own in the big dangerous world? Unlikely, as she's pretty much out of the picture as soon as they step out the door of their house and hear the latch fall back in place behind them, though she does have a lasting influence on how they go about trying to create new homes for themselves. But if not the mother, who else is there? The farmers that the pigs meet along the road and who offer them straw and sticks with which to build their houses? Or what about that third farmer the third little pig encounters, the one who gives him a present of bricks? Even though he features for only a moment in the story, the third farmer's meeting with the third little pig is a world-changing moment in the history of how little pigs disport themselves in the world, for his gift of bricks changes the pattern of pig behaviour and the third little pig, instead of building a house out of organic material (and when you think about it, after straw and then sticks the next logical material should be something like boards or logs) goes and builds a house out of *human-made* material, bricks, and in so doing finds himself protected when the dreaded wolf arrives. He becomes the first pig not to be instantly gobbled up by the wolf. In fact, instead he becomes the first little pig to have the opportunity to consider what the wolf really is and to have the time to think of ways of outsmarting what had, up to now, been a totally superior and unknown enemy.

The acceptance of the bricks from the third farmer by the third little pig obeys the laws of Aristotle's theory of drama because interaction with a third character (the farmer) changes the relationship between the protagonist (pig) and antagonist (wolf). Obviously it changes the relationship, because the third little pig doesn't get gobbled up; in fact …

Let's come at this a different way for a minute. Let's say there's a woman who loves a man who does not love her in return. The woman is our central character (our protagonist); she is the one loving the man, and the man is the second character (the antagonist). Now the woman doesn't have to eat the man, or the man the woman, for them to be protagonist and antagonist; their desires simply have to be in some sort of conflict. But what we're missing is a third character. We have a set-up, of sorts, but little possibility of a climax and therefore no story.

Let's say the woman, Helen, tells her friend Jill about her love because she's hoping Jill will give her advice or help her in her quest. Now we have the possibility of a story. For instance:

(a) Jill gives Helen help and Helen gets her man in the end;

(b) Jill tries to give Helen help but in fact she only makes things worse and Helen fails to get her man;

(c) Jill actually wants the man for herself, and so she purposely spoils Helen's chances.

Obviously there could be many variations on how this will go, some for the better (from our protagonist's point of view, that is) and some for the worse, but simplistic as these plot outlines may seem they do obey Aristotle's theory because the involvement of a third character changes the relationship between the protagonist and second character, the woman and the man.

The Love Triangle. Think about it. All love stories are a triangle of some form or another, or even many overlapping and intersecting triangles, but never parallel lines. Parallel lines never meet, which is hardly going to make for an engaging story. And the Love Triangle works in stories because, however much we might want things to end happily for the protagonist, we want to see love first threatened and then victorious, or maybe we even want to see it threatened and destroyed if that's what makes us feel involved. But, either way, love without threat is dull. Two happy lovers are dull. Romeo and Juliet on their own would be a bore. As would Diarmuid and Gráinne and millions of other star-crossed couples. We need a jealous neighbour, an angry parent, a spurned suitor, a wicked wizard, anything to 'up the ante' and make this love jump through some fiery hoops.

And according to Aristotle, for real drama to occur, the interaction of the third character and the protagonist must be as a result of an action of the protagonist. And this is crucial. It's not enough for the parent of the boy who wants to bring the girl to the disco to say no; the boy must make the mistake of saying *why* he wants to go to the disco, saying *why* he wants to borrow the car. Similarly, in the case of the three little pigs, it's not enough for the third farmer to just give the third little pig some bricks and, hey presto, the wolf is kept out and the pig can get on with living. The pig must *request* the bricks from the farmer. He must be the one who carries out this crucial action, because the story revolves around him. He is the protagonist, the doer and not the done-to. Things might befall him (the bad luck of having an angry parent, or whatever) but he must be, at some level, responsible for his own fate. Otherwise he's just the lucky or unlucky victim of circumstance and not a real player in his own story. The pig must request the bricks, he must take the bricks, he must seal his own fate, for better or worse.

Traditionally speaking, in a story where the protagonist succeeds there is comedy, where he/she fails there is tragedy. The end result is brought about by the character's *own doing*. Put it this way: if a character is killed by a piano which falls from the sky, there is an incident, an amusing anecdote, but no drama, no story. The gods decide to drop a piano and there's a victim but no engagement. However, if it was the same character who originally tied the piano up there – maybe he was doing some furniture removal for someone – and then said, 'Hell, I'm tired. I'd like a break and a cup of tea. It'll do up there like that till I get back from the pub,' and then stepped out on the street only to be flattened by the piano which had been badly secured on its winch, *then* there's the possibility of a story, because the character is involved in his own fate. Events may push a character hither and thither, but the character must make decisions, choices. That is why we want to see what happens. We are not interested in falling pianos in themselves but in the people whose laziness or stupidity causes them to fall, and better still if they fall on those people themselves. In all stories, at some level, we are interested in character. Therefore, before we come back to some of this theory, let's first start our fiction games with a few that will help us to explore the idea of what characters are and how we might work with and develop them.

> ✏️
>
> Take just a couple of minutes and come up with a very general idea for three characters who might be involved in a plot. At this point there's no need to worry about how the plot might work itself out. All we're looking for is a kind of triangle in which three characters, each of whom wants something, are involved.

So we need three characters, at least; obviously we can have lots more, but three at least. (Some people will contend that some of their favourite stories have only two characters or even one character, but let's hold on this for a while until we get this three-part idea clear in our minds.)

Now, the next logical question, once we have three characters to play with, is how do we decide which character is to be our central character, our protagonist, and then which is to be the antagonist and which the crucial third character? Well, remembering that the protagonist (central character) must perform the climax action, as well as the other two main actions of the Plot, we should be fairly readily able to decide which character this will be. If you find this difficult, it might help to imagine that you're looking at the blurb on the back of a book or a video cassette which describes the story. 'This is the story of John, an unemployed dentist who decides to set out for the North Pole and tries to persuade his lover Attila, an Irish-speaking Turk raised in the Connemara Gaeltacht, to accompany him.' Obviously this is going to be John's story, the story of his quest, though equally obviously Attila is also going to feature largely. The third character will now be someone who changes the relationship between John and Attila (for better or worse) because of something John does (seeks this person's help, pushes this person face down in the snow, or whatever).

If all this third character stuff sounds a little cold (no pun intended) and mathematical, let's not forget that the 'system', if we can call it that, is just a way of describing something that most of us know instinctively: it takes two to tango, but three to make suspense and drama. The drama doesn't start when the couple get up to dance, but when the stranger approaches and taps one of them on the shoulder. And even then it doesn't really start until one member of the couple, the protagonist, acts. 'Hey, leave my girl alone!' or whatever is the clichéd requirement to building up to the fist-fight scene. Put another way, if there were just one body in the vacuum of space, as any astronomer will tell you, it would be impossible to say if it were moving because there would be nothing to measure it against. Put in a second body and now we can say that, yes, there is movement, but it's impossible to say *which* of the bodies is moving. In fact, we need a third body to determine this. Just as we need three axes, the x, y and z axes, to describe the location of a body in space, we need three characters to describe (plot) a story.

To further complicate matters, when you think about it each of the characters in a story is a central character in his or her own way, in that each is at the centre of his or her own story. If there are three people in a room and each of them wants something, then each of them will tell a different version of what goes on in the room with him- or herself as central character. For the author, however, there must be a choice between possible central characters because the author will (usually) want the reader to experience the events of the story through the eyes and experience of one of the participants rather than through them all simultaneously. I say usually here because there are exceptions. Sometimes an author will want the reader to sympathise equally with all the characters in a story and so will give each of their points of view in turn, but in fact this is no longer a single story but a number of stories told simultaneously, in each of which there will be a central character, an antagonist and a third character. But before you decide to try to balance that complex of characters, it might be a good idea to first try to make sure you've got a solid grip on the three-part principle of one story at a time.

Clearly, *whose* story you decide to tell determines what *kind* of story you tell. Take the Love Triangle again, this time of two men fighting for the attentions of one woman. (We're not looking for originality here, not yet, just clarity.) If we chose as the central character the man who will eventually lose the woman, clearly the story would be very different than if we had chosen for our central character the man who wins. (Anyone interested in this idea might like to look at Julian Barnes' *Talking It Over*, a novel in which we get to hear each of the involved characters' differing versions of events, with entertaining results.)

So the choice of central character is crucial to the direction of the story. But what makes for a 'good' central character, if any of them might equally well have been chosen? In a word, change. If we see a character change, or face change and fail, we are affected and become involved in his/her experience. A central character has a dilemma, a problem, an obstacle, a challenge to face, and we want to see her succeed, or sometimes fail (after all, she might be a monster!). What gives her depth is that whatever she is like on the outside, in normal daily activity, is not all there is to her. If she is a good, funny, happy-go-lucky person, there is very likely a dark side that certain events might bring out, and if there is the possibility that this dark side will out we will be involved in her story, if only to see will she make it through to the end. A character who is the same all the way through, on the other hand, will appear dull and one-dimensional (remember our x, y and z axes) because we will not be able to register movement and change, and therefore life. If there were a definition of life it might be that *Things Change* (as the title of the David Mamet scripted movie has it). Without change we are looking at stasis, and stasis doesn't hold our attentions or our imaginations for very long.

On the contrary, a central character will be complex (not necessarily to the point of psychosis, by the way!) but sufficiently so that he acts differently in different situations, and there may even be situations where he acts in a manner that is not at all as he would*like* to. Part of the interest of many stories is that the central character gets into a situation in which he or she does not know how to act, or acts inappropriately. At this point the reader's desire and taste for change is whetted. The reader is hooked.

## 'INAPPROPRIATENESS'

*'Reporting the extreme things as if they were the average things will start you on the art of fiction'*
– F Scott Fitzgerald

This notion of something being inappropriate – to time, place or behaviour – is often a great way to kick-start a story. We can see it, for instance, in the way many jokes are built. 'A guy walks into a doctor's surgery with a sausage in one ear and a fried egg in the other ...' Because the situation and the character's behaviour are so at odds, in a single sentence the joke has been set up so that we can already cut straight to the punch line. 'The doctor takes one look at him and says: "It's obvious, you're not eating properly."' On the other hand, if a man goes into the doctor and says, 'I'm ill,' the joke hasn't started to catch our attention at all and demands significantly more in the way of set-up.

But enough theory. Let's try to make a game of this general idea of out-of-placeness, or inappropriateness, and, just as in the doctor's-surgery joke above, we'll resist the temptation to go completely over-the-top with location and instead look for behaviour that is inappropriate in a location we know fairly well.

First of all, let's pick the location. Let's start with something familiar. Let's say, wherever you are, right at this minute.

> ✍️
>
> (a) Write a brief description of the place you are in right now, reading this book. Take no more than five minutes.
> (b) Now consider these questions: what other person doesn't belong there? How would that person behave if they found themselves there with you now? The person could be a thief who walks in while you're reading, a twelfth century knight, a little round grey alien, a former lover, the old man from the shop down the road ... How would they feel? What might they say? What would you do if you turned to find them there?

In the above situation you are taking a place you know, presumably pretty well, and introducing a person who doesn't belong there. The converse of this game is to take a person you know very well, in one or more contexts, and to imagine them in a place they don't know at all, maybe a place they would feel very strange or insecure, but certainly a place where they would be 'out of their element'. Again it is not necessary that this place be outlandish (though go for that if it feels good), but simply somewhere they are not at ease, somewhere where they are what we might call off their home base.

Barry Yourgrau in his wonderful collections of extremely short short stories (*Wearing Dad's Head* and *A Man Jumps out of an Airplane* among them) has perfected the art. 'At night some men are beating an animal down in the garden,' begins the story 'Rite' while 'The Greek' begins, 'I am brushing my teeth at the washbasin when I notice a spear in the bathtub.' Yourgrau plays the idea for comedy and horror, but there are all sorts of other possibilities.

Remember the *Sesame Street* song: *One of these things is not like another, one of these things just doesn't belong ...?* Well, imagine that the thing in question is a person you know, and then put them where they don't belong. The 'little old dear' who stumbles into a pornography shop to ask for directions. Your toddler standing in the middle of an 8-lane highway. Your bank manager suddenly walking in to find you in the bath. Take a few minutes to find a setting and then introduce someone who doesn't belong. Then write just a few paragraphs about what happens, concentrating on the details: what is said, what is done, what actions are or are not taken. (If you find getting physical details down is difficult, try imagining the scene with the sound turned down. In other words, allow yourself to write none of the actual words that might be spoken but instead try to convey what people are feeling by the way they move, their expressions, the gestures they make. Then, when you're happy with the scene, allow yourself to add maybe a couple of short snatches of speech.

Looked at like this, it's possible to find many stories that could begin with the idea of someone who doesn't belong. Think of any number of western stories that begin with the arrival of a stranger in a sleepy Midwest town, or, on a more sublime scale, have a look at Colm McCann's wonderful short story 'A Basket Full of Wallpaper' about a Japanese painter and decorator who conducts his affairs in a sleepy Irish town under the curious eyes of the local youngsters.

All of which suggests our next game.

# VISIBLE AND INVISIBLE

(a) Pick two places you know very well and between which you travel often, preferably on a daily or nearly daily basis. The places should be fairly close to each other, within a couple of miles or so at most. For instance, you might pick the house you live in and the place you work, or the local shop, or a friend's house down the way.

(b) Now try to remember the last time you made the journey from the first to the second, which might be even just earlier today. Imagine you are stepping out from the first on your way to the second. If it might help to close your eyes, do so. It's important to call up before your mind's eye the actual details.

(c) Now, without taking too much time over it or worrying about the importance of it, write down a list of the things you *didn't* see today, the things you *don't* recall, the things you *didn't* notice because you didn't need to notice them, because you knew they were there. Did you actually see the sky today? *The sky! Of course I saw the sky.* I know you know it was there, but did you actually *see* it? Or the lamppost just outside the door, or the fence that needs fixing, or the crack in the path that you always notice (or do you?), or the church down the street? The items on your list might be big objects or tiny objects (the nail that protrudes from the back of the door), it doesn't really matter. What matters is that you write them down and that you do so as if you were actually again, right now, moving from point A to point B, so that you see them in the order in which you did *not* see them.

Now the interesting thing about the existence of such a list (and this game should be performed often if it is to make its point clearly) is that in a sense you *did* see the things, or at least *something* in you saw them. It was just that you didn't have to acknowledge them because you knew they were there and so you were free not to bother about them. (On the other hand, if they had somehow suddenly been absent, you would probably have noticed quickly enough. I didn't notice the door handle when I came back from the loo just now, but if it hadn't been there I imagine I'd have noticed.

We could say that we sense things on at least two levels, the conscious and unconscious, maybe. The things that do not change, or greatly change, move from conscious to unconscious memory; we pay attention, and feel we need to pay attention, only to the unusual. Computers were designed on the same principle. Sort all your work away on the hard disk, and even a small amount of RAM (Random Access Memory) will get you by.

In order to appreciate the possible uses of 'visible' and 'invisible' information, let's go back to our lists again for a moment or start a new pair of lists. Say the 'invisible' items in your list include stairs, door handle, sky, broken tree outside door, shoemaker's sign, etc. Now write down a list of the things that you *did* see, the objects and items you did notice, some of which may never have been there to see before – a particular passing car or person – but many of which will have been there, though they struck you only today for whatever reason. Take a couple of minutes to do this so that you have something concrete to work with later. Again, if necessary, close your eyes and try to take the journey again in your mind, from A to B so that things occur in the right sequence.

Now let's say we're writing a scene in which there are two characters present, one who lives in the particular place where the scene is set, the other who is a stranger. You've probably already guessed how this might connect to our lists. To create the perspective of the local we might do well to lean towards the list of 'visible' things, because for locals certain things tend to become more or less invisible after a while and to dwell too much on the 'invisible' details list betrays the fact that the author is present, suggesting and building up the picture. (In fact, this might well be why so many of us like to show strangers around our towns or cities, as it gives us a chance to see our home places through new eyes and to appreciate them again.) The man living all his life outside Avola in southern Sicily will, to some extent, stop seeing the cacti that line the road to his house, though the Irish tourist who happens to pass by in a car will likely want to stop to marvel at the sheer abundance of so unfamiliar a plant. (Guess where I was on my holidays.) A scene which features a local and a stranger, then, is almost the ideal way to describe a place, and the movement of perspective from one to the other can give a reader a very convincing sense of place and character at once.

It's important to remember here, however, that to formalise this notion might be a big mistake, because mood is also a crucial matter in how a scene is described and how a character relates to it. A character who feels his world falling apart because his wife has just left him should not be denied the possibility of noticing cracks in his footpath just because they have been there for years. In fact, in a particular mood, those same familiar cracks may very well suddenly take on a captivating, almost entrancing aspect.

## VARIETY OF SETTING

Something else that we might keep in mind when considering setting and detail in a story is variety. While it is true that some people spend much of their time in the pub or in the kitchen –

if we are to believe much of what we see on television and in early attempts at stories, at any rate, all human life is conducted there and nowhere else. The truth is, of course, that we spend lots of time in bed, in the bathroom, walking from room to room, climbing stairs, etc., but most of this goes unused. Yet anyone who's suffered those awful postcards where a woman in a flimsy night-dress inadvertently locks herself out of her house in the middle of the night, or those seemingly countless movies about the unusual views offered to window cleaners, doctors and taxi drivers, knows that there are occasions for stories outside of the usual locations too.

Say we have a story about a husband and wife who are fighting a lot. Now it's certainly quite likely that most of the scenes in this story will be set in the kitchen or living room or possibly the bedroom of their house, but how much better and more dramatic one of these scenes could be made were it to be set in the local supermarket on a Saturday morning when the aisles are bursting with the listening ears and prying eyes of neighbours and strangers! And even within the supermarket itself there are lots of possibilities for variety and for 'upping the ante' on the argument in progress. For instance, who is it feels most secure, the wife or the husband, should the argument break out just as they reach the sanitary-towel section?

Conversely (and playing the game of totally turning the tables on an idea is often very rewarding), we expect a wedding to take place in public, in front of invited guests and perhaps the occasional passer-by. But what about this for an opening paragraph?

> 'Do you take this woman et cetera et cetera?' said the reverend Black before turning to spit into the darkness and then wait for the splash maybe ten or fifteen feet below. 'Do you?'
>
> 'Yes,' groaned Watson, the chains digging into his wrists so much that he thought his arms would separate from his shoulders and leave him to fall forwards at the feet of the hideously ugly figure standing to the reverend's right.

Something moved just above his head, maybe a bat, though neither of the two facing him flinched.

There was a hard clicking noise.

'I asked you a question, brother,' said the reverend, who was now holding a pistol aimed directly at Watson's head.

'Yes,' said Watson, wondering how Muriel might ever forgive him, if, of course, he ever got to see her again. 'Yes,' he said, 'yes, I do.'

Looked at like this (and I make no apologies for the stupidity of the above if it helps to make my point), the whole basis for the situation comedies so beloved of television producers becomes evident. Either you take three or more relatively normal people and you put them in an unusual situation, or you take three or more quite abnormal people and put them in a normal situation, or, best of all, a little of each.

## THREE CHARACTERS?

There I go again, saying three characters (at least), first, second and third, but many readers of this book will by now be suffering Aristotle's theory of drama because they'll have seen or at least will be aware of any number of plays like David Mamet's excellent two-hander *Oleanna* in which there are always and only ever the same two characters on stage, or even plays and stories with only one character throughout. So what about Aristotle's theory in cases like this? Was he wrong? Do we throw the theory out and carry on regardless? Not at all. Though it may at first seem like a facile response, the solution is to broaden our definition of what constitutes a character so that it may include other non-speaking figures in the play or story, at times even extending to lifeless objects that *represent* missing characters. Indeed, in considering Greek drama, that band of voices chanting in unison that was the chorus may very easily be seen as a character or 'conscience' or 'culture' and in a sense every character, as we recognise the word, equally stands for a system of beliefs, opinions, hopes and desires.

Anyone who has seen Mamet's *Oleanna* or read the text will be struck by what an important part the teacher John's telephone plays in the action. John has a lot on his mind; he's seeking tenure in the college where he works; his wife, whom we never see, is constantly on the telephone to him about the new house they are trying to close a deal on. And in a sense all of these duties, responsibilities and desires are represented by the telephone into which he periodically speaks (even though we never actually get to hear the voice on the other end and can only guess what it is saying from his reactions to it). If the play is about this middle-aged man's abuse of his position as the teacher of a young woman, Carol (or about Carol's contention of abuse, depending on how you view the play), then the head-to-head meetings between John and Carol, interesting as they are, need a third element to stir things up and to pull John off his comfortable home base.

The invention and spread of the telephone was, like many other systems of communication before it and since, quickly recognised by playwrights and storytellers as a convenient method of introducing second or third characters into situations and scenes where it might have taken two to tango but the tango on its own was in danger of becoming a dance-by-numbers routine.

The reason I haven't spent much time on this business of the alternatives to a living third, or even second, character earlier is that creating drama out of objects, symbols and representations is particularly hard to master. For the moment at least we are better off working with three or more living characters so that we can see it is the relationships between the players (she loves him, but he loves her friend, or whatever) that makes for drama and not just telephones ringing all over the place or, as Hollywood so often seems to believe, car chases, sudden explosions and strippers going through their jaded routines in seedy bars on the outskirts of town.

All of which brings us, neatly I hope, on to our next game:

stories close to home. To start this game, or in fact series of short games, let's first try to do something pretty much impossible. Let's try to write our own autobiography in exactly 100 words, no more and no less.

## 100-WORD AUTOBIOGRAPHY

Here's how it works. Take 10–15 minutes maximum and try to tell your own life story in about half a page (A4) or so, or 150 words approximately. Obviously, even before you begin, you can see that quite a lot is going to have to be left out. Most of us would like our autobiographies to start with something like: 'I was born on the 4th of September 1963 in Portlaoise, Ireland, the fourth of what would eventually be five children to Nicholas and Nancy Boran (*née* Delaney) of 74 Main Street ...' The problem, of course, is that I've already used up almost a third of my total word count allotted for this particular game. Clearly some drastic editing will have to be done. And even before I begin my second attempt, I will have to decide on what will be the important details. Not the easiest of decisions. And there are other concerns, such as those expressed by Ivan Illich and Barry Sanders: 'A chief obstacle to writing a modern autobiography is its ending. How can it end, really, reach its final conclusion, until the writer is dead?' Nevertheless, suspending your disbelief, and remembering that you can always come back and try this at any time you like in the future, let's go.

✍

Taking 10–15 minutes, start right away and write your own 100-word autobiography. When you're finished the first draft, count the words and prune anything superfluous until you arrive at a word count of exactly 100. Why 100? Just to make it difficult.

OK, I'm assuming now that you've got something in front of you; whether or not it's something that you're happy with is another matter, but at least you've got something to look at and examine. So let's see: what do you think are the problems? Probably that so much is missing, so much that makes you what you are, *who* you are, but on the other hand maybe there are one or two telling details that seem true. If you're married or have/had a partner, is that part of the autobiography? Is there any other major change involved, change of place of residence, of job, signs of success or failure at some venture, happiness or illness? Do births, deaths or marriages feature? What kind of things have you recorded? If you were to change the names now (if indeed there are names), what kind of person is described in what you've just written? Better still, what kind of character?

Many of us will feel that, even though we knew we had only 100 words to work with, we threw the net too wide and tried to take in too much, ending up capturing very little that we might say is of our character. As Illich and Sanders describe it, autobiography is certainly a difficult undertaking, but there are other kinds of difficulties involved apart from just the thorny business of endings. Now that we've seen some of the problems in working in such condensed forms, let's look at an alternative approach, an approach that won't necessarily give us a whole lot more in the way of word count but which just might allow us to focus on an essential aspect of story writing, play- and film-making: the building of scenes.

## SCENES 1
### *Watching the Film of Your Life*

If time is limited (which it is for us as individuals at least) and if every life contains the seeds of countless stories, clearly the only way to make stories is to focus on details and events that evoke or suggest more than they can simply describe.

Some people say – and I'm happy to report that I have no

personal experience of this – that close to death the events of one's life rush through one's memory again, almost like the scenes in a film. Because time is limited, and in the case of this next game to 10 minutes, let's watch the film of our early lives flash past and try to scribble down just sufficient notes so that we will be able to discuss and examine the scenes involved later on.

For myself, starting with what is one of my earliest vivid memories and moving on, more or less chronologically, if not necessarily in order of importance, the film-notes that might flash past could look something like this:

1. The day I got my first pair of long trousers (green) while my younger brother was given red.
2. Standing in our back yard in darkness hearing bats overhead.
3. Playing hide-and-seek with my cousin Rosemary: I'm in the press amongst the towels and bags.

And it is this kind of pared-down information we are looking for.

> Take 10 minutes now to come up with short descriptions of as many scenes from your life as you can, not stopping because something seems trivial or apparently meaningless, and also not dwelling too long on any one scene so that it interrupts the flow. If you find it difficult to get going, let the first scene be your first memory and then go on from there with whatever comes into your mind, not worrying if you skip over months or even whole years. Work fast and, if you're going really well, double the time limit to 20 minutes if you like.

The next section of the game in which we'll look at the scene notes produced can be a very interesting and inspiring one for anyone who has not yet found subjects for stories or poems that are sufficiently absorbing. In fact, I'd have to say that for beginning writers or even those with only a passing interest in writing, this game is one of the most illuminating of all those described in this book and one which can provide a great insight into what people see in this whole business of trying to write, even when they may never graduate to the idea of publication.

In case you're interested, the game was suggested to me by a book called *Shyness: What It Is and What to Do About It* by Philip G Zimbardo, which I picked up for a few pence in a bargain box in a second-hand shop a couple of years back, not sure why I was attracted to it. In retrospect now, I see that the whole business of shyness has much to do with self-image and self-description which is one of the truly basic questions for anyone engaged in writing. I make this point here to remind readers that developments and discoveries in one's own creative writing very often come from sources that are not immediately or obviously connected to writing *per se*. For if anything, creative writing is about opening possibilities of connection between seemingly unrelated areas of interest. Anyway, on with the game.

---

✍

Assuming now that you've got your own list before you, let's make a few cursory investigations. First of all, glancing back over the scenes in the list, try to answer the following questions, again without spending too much time on them at this point.

1. In how many of the scenes are you alone?
2. In how many of the scenes are you the person in control of the situation?
3. In how many of the scenes are you the person most definitely not in control?
4. How many of these scenes would you describe as dramatic (whether in a large or small way), and how many would you describe as reflective or something similar?

Let's keep in mind the conclusions we have already reached about story earlier:

> 1. that the story usually centres around a single character or, sometimes, a group of like-minded characters;
> 2. that, according to Aristotle's theory of drama, the main actions in the plot of the story are initiated by the central character, the first two of them involving the second character or antagonist, and the third one involving the third character.

For convenience, and to keep the matter of the story in focus here, let's pretend that all the events/scenes on your list happened in the same 24-hour period, even if they actually span several months or even years. This form of compression will help to give our story (for that is what the accumulation of scenes leads to) a sense of urgency and, most important of all, a sense of unity. And once we are relatively happy that we have mastered the movement from scene to scene and from event to event, we can then easily expand the time dimension of the story (though we should remain careful not to loosen too much the tensions that come about almost naturally when we compress things into a smaller space and time).

At this point, and recalling what we have said about plot and its development, it might be useful to see if we already have the makings of a climax in any of our scenes, in other words if we have a scene which we could use as the third component of the plot and then work backwards to fill in the two preceding steps by choosing from the other available scenes. To see if this is possible, we first need to be happy that we have not only a protagonist (probably yourself), but that we have also an antagonist and that both of these have goals and aims, desires and fears. Bringing these desires and fears together will result in the electricity that leads to story. To put it another way, this electricity between characters is often what will convince us that the characters are real and

alive, as it is in the differences between people that we appreciate most their individuality and so see them as real.
Fortunately, because we have a number of scenes at our disposal, and may require only a few to patch together the elements of a rough plot, we already have sufficient background
material to assist in the 'rounding out' of the characters. Not
every event or scene that we consider will end up in the final
story, but the ones that do must be interesting in themselves
and must, more importantly, contribute to the overall impression made by the accumulation of scenes. A story which
opens with a child feeling jealous because he's been given
green trousers and not red may not seem to be leading anywhere much, but if it goes on to reveal in other scenes the
growth of that jealousy or, on the contrary, the discovery of a
generous side to the same character, then that scene, simple
though it is, contributes to the whole and in fact prepares the
way for the development and change of character that is to
follow. A couple going to the registry office suggests a past
between them that can be alluded to even as they walk up the
steps and in the door.

> They reached the door and stopped. Registry
> Office, the sign read. She found it hard to believe
> the words. Weren't they still just 16 and playing
> about in the field behind the garage? Where had
> the time gone?
> 'You ready?' he said. And she looked and he
> was holding the door open before her. Like a man.
> Like a husband.
> They entered and she was surprised to hear the
> sounds of human voices, laughter, greetings. She
> almost expected to find her father there in his
> overalls, his face and strong arms red from the sun
> and his hands black with oil. Instead she saw her
> sister and her mother, her mother staring straight
> ahead in the vagueness of solitary old age.

We assume they have known each other for some time and have agreed to marry each other. If this is the case, there is not much point in preceding this scene with 39 in which we get to oversee every date the couple have been on, etc. Unless there is some point to be made in doing so, we would be much better off going only for those scenes which have something to do with the Theme of our story. What that might be is only hinted at in each individual scene (after all we are not in the business of delivering lectures in our stories, or shouldn't be). Theme is only really understood by moving from scene to scene towards the story's conclusion.

And there I've brought in another scary word. But when you think about it, theme is little more than the connection between the various scenes and events included in the short-list for your story. The story about the boy with the green, as opposed to the red, trousers might well be an investigation into the theme of jealousy. How this simple discovery differs from the essays we were asked to do in school (and which, if you were anything like me, you hated) is that, because we started with the individual scenes and then looked at them to see how they might connect, we *discovered* the theme as we went along rather than superimposed it from the start. And again, if you're anything like me, you won't want to keep writing day after day if all you're writing are things you already know and believe. If you're not discovering something on a regular basis, like a musician messing about with chords and scales, you're very unlikely to stick at it for the length of time it's probably going to take.

## CHARACTER DEVELOPMENT

Now, let's move on to a couple of games designed to help us develop particularly our central character (so that we will at least have the focus on the story intact). These games can also be used to help to flesh out any other characters deemed necessary to our plot.

To understand fully what is meant by the notion of plot arising out of character rather than the other way around, we have only to think of well-known if by now clichéd characters like the television detective Columbo. Imagine a story in which Columbo is drugged and wakes up to find himself on the moon. It's not very difficult, and the reason it's not very difficult is we know the character so well and once we add a situation (finds himself on the moon) the ideas for plot begin to form themselves almost automatically (though some will obviously be better than others). But if the type of character we choose helps to determine the plot, just what kind of characteristics in our character are most useful? Do we need to know, for instance, his date of birth, his favourite colour, the name of the school he went to? Well, the answer here seems to be no. Literature is full of all sorts of characters about whom we really know very little by way of biographical information (many of Beckett's characters, for instance, seem almost to have no past at all). While this kind of information is often a big help when it comes to fleshing out scenes and conversation and other details that help to keep a reader's interest, it may not be what counts. But if not these kinds of details, then what do we really need to know?

## 'STREET ANGEL, HOUSE DEVIL'

We're all aware of the expression 'street angel, house devil', meaning a person who is one thing in his private life and another thing in public. And here, in a very simplified form, is the essence of what it is we're looking for: tension and conflict. Indeed, it should be relatively easy to see how a character with such opposing faces could be at the centre of any number of plots: the good-time drinker who comes home to beat his wife (too many examples to name); the famous clown who is really a sad and lonely individual (Chaplin's *Limelight* among many others). Now we may not always be happy to settle for such polar and, it has to be said, almost exhausted tensions, but in similar tensions and conflicts the essence of character and therefore plot is often discovered.

How then might we go about looking for tensions within a central character?

Personally, I like the idea that a character begins to come to life when he or she is moved off his or her home base, or out of his or her element, if you prefer, to use an expression I've used before. The lonely man, drawn off his home base, might suddenly find within himself the ability to perform or, more subtly, to teach or lead, while the individual who is constantly nervous in public may have a hobby or calling that helps to earth and centre her. What is important in the theory of plot is that the central character is made up of a variety of elements and desires, desires which drive the plot forward, not always in a straight line, but forward, for better or worse.

Similarly, the central character's weakness is what often brings him to the point of a dilemma in the plot, the point where he turns to the third character and thus creates, consciously or unconsciously, the climax of the story.

Take the typical love triangle again: John loves Mary but Mary takes no notice of him. He tries flowers. No good. He tries singing outside her window. She pours the flower water over him. This will continue until the end of time, with his being constantly rejected, unless he tries something else, something probably unexpected, something that he hopes will take Mary by surprise but will also drag him off his safe home base. Let's say he goes to Mary's friend, Jane, and tells her of his love for Mary. This might well be what it will take to change things. For a start, Jane is herself in love with John. And the fact that John has now told her he loves Mary makes Jane decide to do all she can to separate them for ever. This is clearly the moment of climax in this story, because now almost anything can happen, but it is certain that some change has been set in motion after which nothing will ever be quite the same again. At last John is out of his element, off his home base, veering a little out of control.

If we are familiar with the story of Shakespeare's*Hamlet*, we will recognise Hamlet's killing of Polonius as the climax of the play. Convinced it is his murderous uncle Claudius who is in hiding in his mother's chamber, Hamlet plunges his sword through the arras and kills the wrong man. Hamlet is the protagonist of the play (even the title tells us that), and his uncle Claudius is the second character or antagonist (after all, he is the one Hamlet seems to spend his time watching and spying on, waiting for his moment). And now it is Polonius who becomes the third character, not because he has been given the third most lines in the play or because he is Ophelia's father (though that will obviously have a big influence on Hamlet's relationship with both Ophelia and her brother Laertes), but the real reason that Polonius is the third character of the main plot is because his death lets Claudius know for sure that Hamlet 'is on to him', that Hamlet knows Claudius has killed his father, the late king. The reversal of fortunes that occurs at this moment – up to now Hamlet was stalking Claudius; from now on Claudius will be stalking Hamlet – is a typical indication that the plot has reached its climax.

The hunter becomes the hunted, and all because he has, as it were, shown his hand too early. But what got Hamlet into this almost impossible position in the first place, a position from which, as the play goes on, we see he will not escape with his life? The answer is impetuousness, hot-headedness, rashness, call it what you will. It is something in Hamlet's own character make-up that has doomed him. The question of the play now, after the killing of Polonius, is no longer did Claudius kill his brother, the king (Hamlet's father), and will Hamlet avenge him, but will Hamlet too now die at Claudius' hands?

Will the hero (protagonist, first character) die as a result of an act which arose out of a fundamental aspect of his own nature, or will he come through the wiser for this mistake? Will he now change of his own accord, or will he be changed (killed, in this case)? That is the question. In other words, will this be a tragedy or a comedy, to use the Greek terms to describe the protagonist's fate? In fact the play ends in a blood bath with Hamlet dying, Ophelia already dead by suicide, Claudius dead, Hamlet's mother poisoned, etc. But in terms of the main plot, the difference between comedy and tragedy is whether Hamlet himself survives. Of course, it's also possible that no one at all dies and that Hamlet's tragedy is to be sent into exile or some such punishment. However, to raise the stakes sufficiently to command our undivided attention, the danger of physical pain, loss and even death is very often irresistible.

Indeed, something like this is probably the reason why the writers of the *Superman* comic strips had to invent Kryptonite, the one substance which might destroy Superman. Laboured though it is as a device to show his vulnerability, without it Superman as a central character would literally not be worth bothering about. He would be impossibly and boringly invulnerable, and if there's a rule to be dug out here it is that every protagonist, good and bad, while trying to overcome some obstacle must also himself be in some form of danger, physical or mental. Whether he be trying to win a lover, defeat an enemy or make his new launderette a success, the central character must have something to lose and some weakness in himself that threatens to make that loss come about.

Thus, James Stewart's character in Hitchcock's *Vertigo* battles with a fear of heights while also fighting for Kim Novak's love, and there are a million more examples. Put simply, every Achilles needs a heel of vulnerability.

## THE CHARACTER SEESAW

Let's see now if we can find some way to draw out details of our central character's possible weaknesses and then use some or even many of them to help to drive a plot. The first place to start is with a list of what qualities we think our protagonist may have. In order to make this exercise work and surprise us, we should be careful not to pre-empt a decision on whether qualities are good or bad and simply list neutral qualities and then look at them in different situations. (Some of these qualities may already have been suggested to us by scenes or situations we have come up with before: the older brother who isn't terribly happy that his younger brother gets the desirable red trousers, or whatever.)

Here's an example: John from the John, Mary and Jane love triangle.

*Neutral Qualities*

Focused

Attentive

Quiet

Not terribly interesting qualities for a central character. But now imagine that each of these (relatively) neutral descriptions belongs on the centre of a seesaw, the extreme left of which represents this quality at its worst and the extreme right of which represents this quality at its best. Thus we might end up with something like:

| *Negative* | *Neutral* | *Positive* |
|---|---|---|
| Relentless | Focused | Persevering |
| Obsessive | Attentive | Devoted |
| Sullen | Quiet | Reserved |

As you can see, not all of these examples have worked out very well in suggesting extreme positive and negatives (partly because it's not usual for us to have to try to consider people's neutral qualities, and so we might not get it right the first time). But even out of just these three examples, there is already one which offers some good possibilities for our story. In the second example, Obsessive–Attentive–Devoted, we can see how someone who is attentive might, given the circumstances, either become a devoted partner or an obsessive one. The quality of attentiveness we might call the home base, and now the plot of the story will be developed to show how this person can be coaxed or dragged or teased off his home base towards change. In a word, it is change that is at the centre of all stories, and a game like the above helps us to keep this idea in mind. Incidentally, it is also possible, and perhaps even preferable sometimes, to consider the extreme nature of a character's make-up and then try to work out the other extreme opposite and from these two points map back to the central, relatively stable point. Whatever works for you is the best way to go, but it is always a good idea to have a few possible home bases to be thinking about before you commit to any one of them alone.

> ✍
>
> Take the central character from your own outline plot devised earlier and map out your central character's emotional/psychic seesaw. Make sure to explore even those qualities which at first seem to offer no great possibilities of change.

Once upon a time, all fairy tales begin, things were always the same. The story or drama, however, only commences with 'then one day ...' because that one day is the day that something happened that would *change* things. This is a fundamental feature of all stories, not just that things happen, but also that people change.

## FEAR OF CHANGE

The above game is a very simple and useful way to ensure that both some kind of change and some kind of tension exist in your story. Because the central character, in changing, will lose in one respect and gain in another, he or she is often resisting of that change. People resist losing things they are familiar with, even though these things might be bad for them, and even though they know at the end of the uncertainty of the changing period there will be something new to come. Therefore, a character who seems to change too easily will not be a believable character. As well as change itself, we need to see Fear of Change.

At the same time, the road to change can be very gradual, and it can take people all their lives to change. Unfortunately, the whole of a character's life is pretty certain to be too long a period to try to record in a short story, or even a novel. 'Every day and in every way I get better and better' is the well-known self-improvement mantra popularised by French psychologist Émile Coué towards the end of the last century. In our own case, we might say we're not interested in trying to describe 'every day' but the one day or one minute of that one day when change is at its most dramatic, its most acute and therefore its most visible. What we need to do in a story is 'zoom in' on a particular moment of change where it becomes obvious that the scales have tilted one way or the other, where the central character is moved off her home base. In other words, it's not necessary always to see the drunk downing two bottles of gin for breakfast and then, at the end, chairing the local AA meeting (though such things might conceivably happen). Instead, we can look for a moment, often in a single scene, which the earlier part of the story leads to.

## NEWSPAPER CLIMAX GAME

We looked earlier at the possibility of finding the necessary change in our central character by starting at one or other extreme of his/her emotional seesaw and then trying to figure what it might take to have her move in the opposite direction. When it comes to plotting, there is a similar game we might play. If we are agreed that the climax of a story will be the most dramatic part, and hopefully the part that most stands out in our minds because of its appealing to our various

senses (we'll look at this notion in a little while), might it not
be an interesting game once in a while to try to find a scene
which would make a good climax for a story and then try to
work out what the main preceding actions of the plot of this
story could be? Try this game.

---

✍

1. Find yourself a newspaper and, skipping the
main stories, go directly to those short snippets,
often called News in Brief or set off from the rest of
the page in a little box, and pick one that most
intrigues you. A recent newspaper that I find in my
kitchen offers a report about a man killed by a
lawnmower, two brothers who, after sex changes,
are now two sisters and a report on a weeping statue in the south of Spain.

2. Now, imagine this snippet contains the material
for the climax, rather than the opening of your
story. Because it's the climax (the involvement of
your central character/s with a third character/s),
you now have to figure out what the previous
parts of the story might have been. If John (from
our love triangle) was the man killed by the lawnmower, did he go to Jane's house on the pretext of
borrowing it, and did Jane doctor it so that he
would be killed? Why did our brothers from the
second story have their sex changes? Who performed the operations? And, for our third story,
what has happened earlier in this quiet Spanish
village that has resulted in the statue weeping or
being made to weep? What are the events leading
up to the climax?

---

# ACTIONS SPEAK LOUDER

Here's another short game that can often help with characterisation.

> ✍
>
> 1. Make a list of ten 'good' and ten 'bad' things you've done, that is the ten things you are ashamed or guilty of, and ten you feel happy to remember. The ten bad things must have been things which you were aware were bad at the time. It is not, for instance, of much use to include something you did for all the right reasons but which later backfired on you or on someone else. The list should be made up of events that are not completely moral, right or fair and from the recent past (say the last 12 months). They by no means have to be of enormous significance, however. Indeed they can be so trivial that they seem almost not worth putting in the list.

For example, the list might include something like 'I stole a bar of chocolate in the shop' or 'I jumped the bus without paying the fare' or 'I told a lie to my best friend'. Things that seem of no great importance in themselves, but which you carry with you anyway. The list of good things might contain some which appear equally trivial. 'I sent an old friend a birthday card' or 'I gave someone my ticket to a rock concert because he was really much more interested in the show than I was'.

Two lists of ten things, then, and, as always with these list games, speed is of the essence. The first ten things to come to mind, trivial or not, that's what you want for each list. At different times there can be different lists. What you want now is the list of this moment.

2. Now that you have the two lists before you, and before the game makes itself seem impossible to play, we will shift into second gear, onto the second level. On this level take a pen and, going back through your lists, mark out the main action performed by you in each item. To do this what you have to look for is usually the main single verb. (It may be the case, of course, that you need not only a verb but the accompanying noun so that the thing makes sense. In the case of 'I told lies to my best friend', the whole phrase 'told lies' would need to be included, as the word 'told' on its own does not convey the essential deception.

3. The third stage of the game is one in which we take this second list of verb-based items and, again as quickly as possible, translate these verbs into nouns which describe the perpetuator of such actions. The verb 'stole' in the second list, for instance, becomes the noun 'thief' in the third list, while the phrase 'told lies' becomes the noun 'liar' and so on. It is important to do this quickly and not get bogged down, and it may even be useful to 'translate' an item from each list alternately, rather than to do a whole list consecutively. This way we are far less likely to reach value judgements while the game is still on-going.

4. At the conclusion of this game you now have before you two lists, based upon your own perhaps even random memory, but which at some level describe a number of the 'characters' who go to make up your own psyche. Because of the game you have, at least, been able to admit to and objectify their presence, and while in daily life I might not see myself as a thief, the fact that I picked that particular phrase reminds me that there is this aspect to my make-up and therefore this possibility of conflict in my character.

Conflicts, it should be remembered, come out of all sorts of oppositions and not just polar oppositions. The recognition of these oppositional aspects of the psyche is not only the path to maturity, but also the path into good material for stories. The items in these lists are ways to see ourselves as we are generally seen only by others and even then only in specific situations. By objectifying them like this, we are now able to see them as stories within ourselves and to see ourselves in turn as parts of a greater story.

Indeed, many of the games in this section are intended to help us to see ourselves and our characters as part of more than just one story at a time. Our responses to the way a story is framed or set up helps the author to determine the way in which we will react to character. Compare, for example, these two approaches to telling the story of Ludwig Wittgenstein. Here's the first, quoted directly from the entry on the philosopher in the *Wordsworth Dictionary of Biography*:

> Wittgenstein Ludwig 1889–1951. Austrian philosopher. *Tractatus Logico-Philosophicus* 1922 postulated the 'picture theory' of language: that words represent things according to social agreement. He subsequently rejected this idea, and developed the idea that usage was more important than convention.

And here's the second:

> Once Upon a Time there was a man in Austria called Wittgenstein who had a son whom he decided to call Ludwig, which, in Old German, means the famous warrior ...

Clearly the first version gives us far more by way of 'information' on our character and his work, but the second version, for all its flaws as journalism, does get us very quickly into the realm of story. The fact that we are told his name means warrior in Old German sets a level of expectation that already begins to suggest a direction for our story. Will Wittgenstein have to battle against accepted authority? Will he have to struggle to make his ideas heard and have them accepted? The answer might well be, 'No, in fact he will prove to be totally self-effacing and not at all warrior-like,' but even this possibility relates to the suggestions of our opening.

The part of the reader or listener that responds to story, we might say, is the sense of play; the part that responds to lectures, if anything does respond, is the sense of duty and effort. This is so obvious that many educational establishments have managed to forget it. (The visible has become invisible; the seen has become the unseen). When it comes to character, the only way we can manage to bring our writing alive is to experiment with different approaches, to take risks and, as often as possible, to make mistakes. If we were to decide to study music, how much less appealing might it be if we did not, even occasionally, get to play an instrument?

# SCENES 2

But all this business of large-scale change is only one way of looking at the necessary ingredients of a story. Another way to think about what stories need is to try to focus on creating credible if not necessarily realistic snapshots of life. If something manifests life it will obviously manifest change (the two terms are interchangeable). And to show change we need to show Before and After. A photograph of a short, pudgy man beside a photograph of a tall, muscular man, that is difference. Change is when it's the *same man.* So we need a scene or picture of the man Before the change, and we need another of him After. This seems much more interesting than just seeing the fat, pudgy man and hearing him say he's going to change. And it's also more interesting than seeing the thin, muscular man and having him tell us how out of condition he used to be. We want to *see* change. We want to judge for ourselves.

Scenes in fiction are all about letting the reader judge for herself. The author can tell you, 'Sorry, John is ill.' But it's far more affecting to go right inside John's room and find him lying on a dirty, damp mattress and barely covered with an old woollen blanket while the pillow around his head is damp with sweat. 'Ill?' you feel like saying to the author. 'If I hadn't come in here, this man might have died!'

The difference between the way the information of John's condition was related in the first version and in the second is that the first makes no use of the primary way in which human beings experience the world: through the senses.

## APPEALING TO THE SENSES

Edward James Muggeridge was born in 1830 and died in 1904, a forgotten man. For it was only after he changed his name to Eadweard Muybridge that he began taking photographs of animals in the United States in the 1870s, photographs which were to have a huge influence not only on photography, but also on natural science. Among the things discovered through Muybridge's photographs, taken in rapid succession, was that when a horse gallops, its two left and right legs work in pairs, rather than its front and back. Up to the photographs being taken, this fact had been invisible to the human eye and indeed painters and artists had actually painted horses running with their legs in quite impossible positions.

But if Muybridge's photographs were about a way of bringing the invisible into visibility, so too is creative writing. Stories, poems and plays all attempt to explore emotions and feelings, things which are in themselves invisible. In order to render these qualities in a way which readers, listeners and viewers can relate to, the creative writer needs to find a way to make them accessible to the senses.

Scenes are about senses. We see people and places, we hear conversations, we sometimes even get to taste or touch or smell things and we get to make up our own minds *This man could have died!*

Often the fastest way to discover how John feels is to ask him or to have someone else ask him. Even as a character walks onto the stage at the beginning of a play, and finds himself among three strangers, and wanders slowly across the stage, and goes to sit down, but then doesn't, in fact just stands there, staring, the audience is willing him to speak.*Say* something! How long the playwright leaves him there without having him speak has to do with how much the playwright thinks he can pull on our sense of curiosity before inflaming our sense of impatience. Because we want to hear him. And we want to hear him, not only because we hope a question or two from him will help to establish where he is and who the other people are and what this play is going to be about, but also because we are curious as to what he is like. What kind of character is he? What's his angle? What's his history? What kind of accent has he? How does he relate to the others? What mood is he in? What role is he playing? The answers to many or all of these questions will come only when we hear him speak, even if, in the most surrealist fashion, what he says has no apparent meaning at all. Let's 'produce' this very short scene as if it were a play, just to give us a chance to see it alive, off the page.

MAN (WHO IS CALLED ROBERT) STANDS
FACING ONE OF THREE OLD MEN ON
THE STAGE, GARRICK.

ROBERT (Bewildered)
Antelopes. They said there would be antelopes.
(PAUSE) (SHOUTS) Happiness is! Eh? Remember
that? The face on the train? Remember that?
Happiness is!

GARRICK
We have not made these beds that the river sleeps
in, Robert.

ROBERT
(ALMOST HYSTERICAL) The river doesn't sleep!
Nothing *sleeps!* (CALMS DOWN) I want to go back
to where it was, well, different. Surely you can
understand that? (LOOKS TO OTHERS IN TURN.
WHISPERS) You were me once. You can't just
convince yourselves that that's fiction. You *know*
you can't.

Now, let's forget for a minute that the above is rubbish just
intended to show that even meaningless dialogue can be suggestive for the way in which it is delivered (Robert shouts or
whispers etc.). But then let's consider what else we might add
to the scene, without adding any more dialogue, to increase
this suggestive value, to increase the tension. The answer is
movement. What are they doing while they are speaking or
when they stop speaking? In the following, additions to our
previous version appear in bold type.

MAN (WHO IS CALLED ROBERT)**SUDDENLY
STAMPS OVER** TO FACE ONE OF THREE OLD
MEN ON THE STAGE, GARRICK.

ROBERT (Bewildered)
Antelopes. They said there would be antelopes.
**(HE TURNS AND APPEARS ABOUT TO LEAVE
BUT THEN RUSHES TO THE FRONT OF STAGE.
ABSTRACTLY)** Happiness is! Eh? **(HE RUNS
BACK OVER TO THE OLD MAN AND GRABS
HIM BY HIS LAPELS)** Remember that? The face
on the train? Remember that?**(LETS GO THE OLD
MAN WHO SITS CHOKING. TO HIMSELF)**
Happiness is!

GARRICK
We have not made these beds that the river sleeps
in, Robert.

ROBERT

(ALMOST HYSTERICAL) The river doesn't sleep!
Nothing *sleeps*! (**PACES AROUND**. **STOPS**. CALMS
DOWN) I want to go back to where it was, well,
different. Surely you can understand that? **TURNS**
TO OTHERS IN TURN. WHISPERS) You were me
once. You can't just convince yourselves that that's
fiction. You know you can't.

And while we're adding movement, let's also try adding a few
other suggestive details that will give us hints of the position
in society or the level of power of some of our characters.
Even just the first speech should give the general idea.

MAN (WHO IS CALLED ROBERT), WEARING A TATTY
DENIM JACKET, SUDDENLY STAMPS OVER CENTRE
STAGE TO FACE OLDEST OF THE THREE OTHER MEN,
GARRICK, A SMALL BESPECTACLED FIGURE WITH A
SMALL BLACK HAT AND LEANING HIS CHIN ON A CANE.

Now, it's clear that there's a limit to how far a playwright
should go in matters such as including physical details of characters and setting (after all, having a character who the script
says must be nine-foot tall is going to mean the play is unlikely to be performed very often). Playwrights have to work with
directors and actors and each of these are contributors to the
look and feel of the overall production. But fiction writers
have no directors or actors to carry their scenes. Instead they
have to provide the kind of information that the actors and
director would impart. Unlike the playwright, they will not
often be happy to tell their stories through dialogue and bare
details of movement alone. And at the same time they are
unlikely to resort solely to descriptive detail and authorial
comment (exposition) to drive their stories.

Clearly, some kind of balance is required here and it might
be a good idea to see what kind of things happen to scenes
when the author experiments with switching between a number of aspects of fiction writing to evoke one or more of the
'senses' of her audience.

# SWITCHING APPROACHES

In creative writing workshops one of the most common difficulties people seem to have is that early versions of their stories tend to begin with a mass of description and exposition
(the revealing by the author of the situation as it stands), and
then, when the story starts to find some energy, they suddenly
move into long scenes of dialogue and then they come to an
end. It's as if, instinctively, most people realise that dialogue
raises dramatic tension. After all, when you're speed-reading
that half-interesting novel, the dialogue is usually the bit you
skip to over the ten pages of description that preceded it, and
not the other way around. Every reader knows that, most of
the time, the real drama is going to be in those scenes where
there's dialogue. Once the descriptive stuff has been done and
we know the colour of the heroine's eyes and a fair bit about
the hero's upbringing and how he has always felt the need to
travel the globe looking for a woman with such eyes, such
penetrating blue eyes, we want to hear them speak. 'You're an
idiot, John.' 'I know. I just can't help myself.' 'Well, you'd better learn to because I've just called security to throw you out
of this paragraph, you bastard.'

But the solution of breaking the story into two like this –
first-half descriptive/reflective, second-half dialogue/action –
simply cuts it in half and kills it. Instead we should be looking
to animate the texture of the story with variety, because the
truth is that the *combination* of these things – description, exposition, dialogue, etc. – is what makes scenes appear to have life,
and while different scenes will lean on these aspects in different measure, the majority will contain something of each.

Think about it: when you are in a physically busy situation
you reflect less. How many players in a World Cup Final are
really thinking of the days when they were boys dreaming of
such glory? Very few, during the match at least, but there's a
good chance that some of them were thinking exactly like that
on the way to the game, or in the showers, or, even more
likely, as they stepped out of that tunnel for the first time and

the roars of the crowd went up. *If those guys in school could see me now ...*

What I'm getting at here is that there are places that seem more natural than others for reflection and places that seem more natural for action. If we were to have a rule of thumb here, a good one might be that in most stories reflective, static passages (people staring into fires thinking, etc.) should be earned by balancing them with plenty of scenes with action, whether that action be a detailed difference of opinion about knitting patterns or a fully fledged shoot-out. And better still if the knitting or the shoot-out can help to draw on the qualities of our central characters.

So let's say we go along with the idea that scenes have a number of different possible components. How can we know in what proportions to combine them to make a scene, or a series of scenes, interesting and varied enough to keep a reader's attention? Well the answer here is obviously connected with that word 'varied'. When you think about, a reflective scene is very likely to have quite a bit of physical detail in it – when you're relaxing in front of the fire you notice that cobweb that's probably been there for months, and it sets you thinking on ... But in the middle of a break-in, when there's a stranger in your flat trying to wallop you over the head with one of your own saucepans, you're unlikely to notice that spider web and start thinking about how life too is a strange and wonderful construction.

It's important to remind ourselves that we're not looking for absolute rules about such aspects of story-making (one invents one's own rules by adapting, stealing, mixing. W Somerset Maugham said: 'There are three rules for writing a novel. Unfortunately, no one knows what they are.') What we're looking for are just clear rules of thumb by which we might become familiar and learn to experiment with a variety of approaches. If we feel we have a 'good ear for dialogue' we might also keep in mind that dialogue is not the only tool available to us, and if our scenes tend to appear one-dimensional it may well be that we have forgotten to paint in sufficient physical detail to make our characters and their existences credible.

With this in mind, let's now, and in no particular order, take a quick look at what we might call the five main ingredients of a scene.

1. Character description
2. Location/setting description
3. Dialogue – monologue – speech
4. Exposition
5. Symbol

## CHARACTER DESCRIPTION

Character description at its simplest is writing which draws the reader's attention to the physical make-up, and through that to the psychic make-up, of a character. 'His hair was red' is very basic character description. But 'he was happy' is not character description at all. 'John was seven-foot tall and had blue eyes' is also character description, and a little better than our first example, but still it's not very good. It tells us John's height and the colour of his eyes, certainly, but it wastes an opportunity to show how these physical attributes affect him in the course of his daily life. In fact, as character description goes, it's not much better than a police-department identity photograph, because it isolates John from the world. It shows him in captivity, out of the world, in the abstract.

Compare it to:

> John had to bend down to enter the room, even though the doorway was more than six feet high. When Mary spoke to him she was struck by his blue eyes, unusual for a southern Italian.

No Booker Prize for that, I'm afraid, but at least now we've got something physical about John, *plus* we've got him in some kind of action (entering a room) and we've used the colour of his eyes as a way into divulging the information that he's from southern Italy, *plus* we've got Mary into the scene. In other words, we've brought the description to something approaching life.

This idea of linking character description to action and movement is not always so easily done as here, and again is not intended as an absolute rule, but it is one way of usefully breaking up dull and lifeless paragraphs of description so that they at least have a grounding, a setting, a context.

Consider the following:

> Mary opened the door. The man standing there before her was maybe seven feet tall, tanned, with blonde wavy hair and blue eyes. His mouth was wide and his skin looked fresh and reminded Mary of the beach in southern Italy where she had been lying only days before in the warm sand and feeling stupid because she was wondering if she would ever find the man of her dreams. And now here he was standing before her, his shirt etc.

How long is Mary standing in that doorway? Actually just 80 words long, but 80 words that describe memories and thoughts which suggest she was there for an inordinately long period. In fact, I want Mary to just open the door, see the man and that's it. That's really all I want in this particular scene, now that I think about it. In fact, I'm sure I would be much better off having the man come in and go to the television and be examining it (for that is why he's come, I should have said), and then have Mary starting off on her line of thinking about love or whatever. The problem is not necessarily *what* Mary is thinking (though it's pretty dull stuff) but *when* she appears to be thinking it in our scene. In the way it is represented here, it's not *true* to the situation.

However, if we had written something like the following, the scene might be far more believable.

Mary opened the door. The man standing there before her was maybe seven feet tall. Mary started with fright. He loomed above her. And he was tanned, with blonde wavy hair and blue eyes she could hardly look at. The shock of finding him there like that made her want almost to run, to disappear.

'I've come about the television set ...'

'Yes, yes,' she said, half-stumbling back into the dowdy brown hallway where the bulb was blown and the children's coats hung on the end of the banister like smelly old sheepskins. How was she dressed? She could hardly remember and was afraid to look down.

They entered the living room. How they got there she had no idea. Had she come in first and he followed her? Had someone closed the door? She was staring at the television set and then realised how stupid she must have looked, so she turned around. He was like a living statue of bronze. His mouth was wide and his skin looked fresh and reminded Mary of the beach in southern Italy etc.

The writing's still not great here, and I'm starting to fall back into the dull old static description routine there towards the end, but some of the earlier part has definitely got a little more life, because we're seeing things (having things described) both when we can actually see them and take them in through Mary's eyes *and* when Mary is acutely aware of them because of what is going on (the dead bulb, the heap of coats would likely have been invisible if the caller at the door were just one of her kids).

In fact, this scene is based *very loosely* on a famous early scene from Flaubert's *Madam Bovary* in which Charles (a doctor) comes to treat a Monsieur Rouault who has been involved in a minor accident. When Charles reaches the Rouault household, the door is opened by a 'young woman, wearing a dress of blue merino adorned with three flounces' and that is all we 'see' of her. In fact, it is only when Charles has tended to his patient and he is waiting for the young woman, Emma, to complete her work on bandages and pads for her father's wounds that Charles begins to notice her charms. Actually what happens is she pricks her fingers with a needle and puts them to her mouth, which draws Charles' attention to her. 'Charles was surprised at the whiteness of her nails,' begins Flaubert's next paragraph, and from the nails he guides Charles' (and our) eyes to Emma's hands and then to her eyes. A couple of paragraphs later he begins on the subject of Emma's neck and her hair, though by this stage we have got the point: Charles is smitten. But there is another, more important point: Flaubert gives us the description of Emma gradually, interwoven through the action of the scene and not all in one undigested block. Charles' 'discovery' of Emma's beauty provides a basis for and counterpoint to the action.

The lesson here is that we notice physical details about each other not all at once in a photographic manner (at least the vast majority of us don't), but little by little, with distinct individual impressions coming together to form a composite image.

The fact that we don't always have control over every aspect of our expressions or movements suggests that a study of them might prove rich territory for a fiction writer. Peter Collett, best known as the resident psychologist on Channel 4's *Big Brother,* in his *The Book of Tells* draws attention to what he calls micro-tells, those unintentional giveaway signs that expose what a person is really thinking or feeling as they try to present themselves in a particular way. 'When we're concealing our thoughts,' Collett writes, 'or a particularly strong image enters our minds, it sometimes shows on our faces or in our movements. As soon as the wayward thought has managed to sneak on to our face, the processes that control our demeanour spring into action, remove it and reinstate the desired expression.' But in those couple of moments are rich pickings for the fiction writer.

# MENTAL PHOTOGRAPHS

Try this game.

> 🖎
>
> Go to some public place, close your eyes for a few moments and try to describe to yourself the clothes and physical features of the people around you. Chances are you will be a little less than sure about certain details. OK, some of us are more perceptive than others, but very few have photographic recollection, and photographic description in a story, for this very reason, is surely just as irritating and 'untrue' as hopelessly vague description or no description at all.

# BODY LANGUAGE

Consider for a moment the area of body language. 'She ran her hand through her auburn hair.' 'Her green eyes flashed like emeralds.' 'His piercing blue eyes seem to penetrate to her very soul.' Any of these sentences might have been lifted directly from a real writing workshop story in progress, and they're obviously bad, but why? OK, they're clichéd, but that's not what we're looking at here, at least not just now. Our quibble with them is that they fail totally to bring the owners of these organs to anything approaching life. Let's imagine that we're trying to write one of those scenes in which star-crossed lovers spend an amount of time in silence looking at each other. For some reason, we believe our story needs this. How do we pull it off?

Well, let's say that, as a working rule for this game, every time eyes or hair are mentioned (to name just two of the most common culprits of bad character description writing) we must

delete them completely and introduce some alternative character detail or some piece of dialogue or symbol or detail of
location that imparts the mood we are trying to make in a different way, and aimed at a different one of the reader's senses.

## SUBSTITUTING DIALOGUE
## AND CHARACTER DESCRIPTION

Here's another game.

Take the following scene and rewrite it without the
dialogue. Add whatever further physical description
(location or character) you feel is necessary to
make the scene have the same 'meaning'.

John sat down beside Mary.
'I'm sorry,' he said.
'You're not sorry,' said Mary. 'And I'm still
leaving you. As for your ring, you know what
you can do with it.'

Or take any scene from any story you can find anywhere,
preferably one with lots of speech, and see what happens
when you remove the speech and what kind of physical
details might restore at least some of the meaning. When
beginning writers talk about not knowing what to write about,
they might be well advised to play a version of this game (turn
dialogue into description, turn description into dialogue, etc.),
because often only in such experiments do we begin to understand what kind of writing is effective in which kind of scene.

# LOCATION

Many of the points I would make about details of location have already been made in the section called Visible and Invisible. The notion that there are things with which we are so familiar that they have become invisible is one which should inform our approach to location description. There is also the related difficulty of compression: we have only so few words or so little time to describe a place, what do we select for description? When we went into John's room and discovered him ill, we made straight for the mattress and then the woollen blanket. We didn't start with the colour of the wallpaper, though we might have if that had been the striking thing. The fact that we started with the mattress got us straight to John, the reason we entered the room in the first place, and so gives the reader a hint of our feelings, our desires. To stop and spend time describing the wallpaper would have suggested very strongly that we couldn't give a damn about John. And now that we have made it to John's bedside and discovered that yes he is ill and very ill, but he is still alive, we might now momentarily relax and notice that the reason we saw nothing much else in the room was because the curtains are pulled. Even though it is the middle of the day! So we get up, move to the window and open them.

> The late July afternoon light filled the room, or more correctly it seemed to open it out from the little cave of visibility that had hung over John's bed when I entered into the squash-court sized and almost equally bare chamber in which I now found myself.

OK, this is a pretty unrealistic example of how we might then go on to have a second run at describing the room in which we found John, but it is unbelievable not because it is unlikely (which it is) but because we do not believe it *with our senses*. When the reader opened the door to John's room in the first place, even in the dark she should have felt there was something strange about it. She should have noticed, as she ran to John's bedside, that her footfalls were echoing unnaturally, that the room was colder than one might expect of a bedroom, etc. First we establish the location then, when we have earned some breathing space, we give those descriptions which help to make it feel real. 'It was a very big room the size of a squash court' has less effect on the senses than that moment when the reader opens the door and feels that strange echoing coldness and maybe the smell of sweat and physical exertion. Because, as she crosses to John's bed, the reader still does not know what this means, you can be sure you have her undivided attention.

And while we're on the subject of location description, we might also remember that description is most effective when it is combined with action. a) 'The bottle on the table was blue.' b) 'He picked up the bottle and smashed Carruthers on the side of the head. An explosion of blue dust and Carruthers fell to the ground, his fingers grasping the linen tablecloth to bring the glasses and opener, the two bowls of spaghetti and bread tumbling to the floor.' And the more descriptive detail you feel is necessary, the more you have to earn it by creating a sense of movement. If two people are in a gallery looking at a painting for twenty minutes, the reader will probably go to the pub. As Robert Louis Stevenson said: 'No human being ever spoke of scenery for above two minutes at a time, which makes me suspect that we hear too much of it in literature.' What the author has to do is make what they're saying, what they're doing, in front of that painting so interesting that she can take us all the way through the history of art without losing our attention for a moment.

# DIALOGUE

'Welcome to Dialogue. We've already talked a bit about dialogue.'

'Have we?'

'I beg your pardon?'

'I said, "Have we?" I don't remember.'

'Well we have. You mustn't have been paying attention.'

'I don't remember anything about it.'

'I said it gives a story a sense of movement, of action, of –'

'Ah, yes. Tension.'

'Tension. That's right.'

'Yes. Now I remember. But I'm still not convinced.'

If dialogue is anything, it's the place where the author gets out of the way and lets the characters at it, so to speak. It's the place, too, where we get to see (or hear, really) the inequalities of the various characters: who's in control of the situation, who's feeling pressure, who's telling lies or struggling for words. It's interesting even to listen to conversations between strangers and try to tell, from the length of the speeches alone and their manner of delivery, who is the dominant player in the relationship. In fact, let's imagine that we're working on a scene that lacks a punch. We might consider starting it with dialogue to see if that helps to locate the drama.

But what I want to do now is introduce a game that should give us a clearer sense of how dialogue relates to action in a scene.

# THE RIDICULOUS 'NO NO NO NO NO' GAME

Below are five words, all of them the word 'no', and they represent a short piece of dialogue stripped down to its absolute minimum and devoid of any kind of 'stage directions'.

No

No

No

No

No

What we must imagine is that there are two people in dialogue in this scene, and that the first person speaks the first no, the second speaks the second, the first then speaks the third and so on. If this were the typescript of a play or film it might look like this:

John: No

Mary: No

John: No

Mary: No

John: No

Not the most developed or interesting piece of dialogue ever (though it certainly seems to have plenty of that crucial ingredient of a good story, conflict). What's wrong is that I've given no information on *how* the words are delivered, or what *actions* if any are being performed *while* they're being delivered, or what the *context* or even the *location* of the exchange is. For instance, are the words spoken as questions, statements, exclamations, etc? Are these two people arguing for their lives or just over whether a spider will walk up or down a wall?

But what might we be able to do for such a limited scene if we were to allow ourselves to develop it by adding, wherever we think appropriate, descriptive information on character or setting, say even just two sentences of exposition and maybe a little hint at symbol somewhere, just to give the scene a bit of resonance beyond itself.

You might start with something like: 'No!' Mary exclaimed. And then go on to describe what she was doing or where she was before reporting on what the other person in the scene is at. On the other hand, you might prefer to start off with a couple of lines of character or location description and then interrupt the scene with the first element of the dialogue. There are many ways to approach this.

> ✍️
>
> Try it now, taking 10 minutes or so. No No No No No. Flesh this scene out, adding nothing else by way of dialogue. Then we'll look at ways to examine and hopefully improve the results.

You might have come up with something like the following:

> John opened the door and walked into the room.
>
> 'No!' Mary exclaimed.
>
> John froze as if he had been struck by a wet fish. 'No?' What was she talking about? Just two minutes before she had asked him to make the tea.
>
> He proceeded into the room and then stopped. In the almost darkness of the room, Mary was holding something out to him. The film! Damn! He had forgotten to hide the film before she arrived. He reached out to take it from her and managed to spill the tea.
>
> 'No,' she said, pulling back, moving to the wastepaper bin, the film held out before her towards the light. He had screwed everything up again, as he had every time he tried to do anything

on his own. He had left it there for her to see, and now she had seen, and now she knew.

He followed her over to the window, determined to snatch it from her. He grabbed her arms roughly but then, from her shocked expression, he realised he had over-reacted. He had not stopped first to think. How could it have been*his* film, for *his* film was surely still where he had left it, upstairs, hidden. It must have been some other film! He had over-reacted. She knew nothing whatsoever about the other woman!

He released his grip suddenly and she scrambled back and away from him, allowing the film to fall to the floor so that he knew he was right in his conclusions.

He looked up to find that she was aiming a gun at him.

'No?' she said.

Should he run? Could she really fire? Was she just trying to frighten him? Surely she knew this was all just a joke.

'No,' he mouthed softly. He stared into her big brown eyes, dark around the sockets as he had never seen them before. They stood there like that for a whole minute, neither of them speaking, and then she said, almost to herself, 'No,' and put the gun down on the sideboard. And he moved over to the open window to embrace her, stepping over the film which like a serpent rustled to life in the breeze.

I'm afraid I can't resist this kind of tacky stuff at the moment, but I trust you get the point. Even with the ridiculous limitations imposed by this kind of dialogue, there's conceivably a way to sharpen (if not to make actually usable) this kind of scene. And if we were now to allow ourselves to go back and slightly tweak the dialogue to make it more interesting, we might even manage to make an adequate scene out of even this unpromising original material.

While we're on the subject of dialogue, we might mention too the opening of Roddy Doyle's novel *The Snapper* which is a marvellous example of how dialogue can immediately bring a scene, indeed a whole novel, to life. In fact, in the opening of the book Doyle unusually forgoes establishing shots (description passages) and instead launches directly into dialogue that immediately catches our attention. If the above 'No No No No No' game seems a laboured way of establishing tension, look how effective Doyle's opening speech is.

– You're wha'? said Jimmy Rabbitte Sr.

For a start it tells us that the character who is speaking is surprised. So we know something important has already happened. We are thrown, as the Romans would say, *in medias res*, into the middle of things. It tells us he is probably from Dublin (the accent is hinted at) and probably of 'working class'. It tells us, obviously, that he is talking to someone else and, from the direct manner of his question, probably among friends or family. It tells us too that he is a parent and that he has a son called Jimmy. A lot of information and a lot of suggestion. Which is pretty impressive as an opening, considering Doyle has used only two words of actual dialogue, plus a single (and single-syllable) verb and the speaker's name! If writing is about precision, there's a lesson here for us all.

# EXPOSITION

Exposition is a harder one to define. It's background, information, psychology and a whole lot of other things. One definition of it might be those things which are told and not shown. Mary had been to school in London for a year when she was 21. That's exposition. It could also be dialogue. 'Hi, Mary,' said Louise, Mary's friend at the new job. 'You went to school in London, didn't you?' 'Yes, Louise, until I was 21,' Mary said like a robot and then there was a whirring noise and she fell to the ground like the automaton that she was.

My point is that, while it's sometimes possible to cut down on the need for huge tracts of exposition by working some of the material into dialogue, there's a danger that you'll end up with characters who speak in completely unbelievable ways, like Mary above. Again, exposition is something that we might think of as having to be earned. If we have to take a detour and explain something about a character's past, we might try breaking it up into manageable lumps for a start.

Here's an interesting experiment we might try (and it's essentially the same game we've played earlier substituting dialogue for description).

> Take a passage of exposition from a familiar novel and try to write a scene with dialogue and movement to convey as much of the expository information from the passage as possible. Try to keep your characters speaking in a believable way.

# SYMBOL

When we come across a symbol in a story we come across two things, the thing itself and the thing evoked. Let's go back to the scene in which John and Mary argue, and John almost gets shot, for the roll of film. At the end of the scene, John steps over the roll of film which is compared to a serpent. Is this the serpent in the Garden of Eden? Is this the serpent time, or the Ouroboros, the mythological serpent who, encircling the world, eats his own tail? Of course it is none of them exactly, because this story is set in the present and has nothing to do with mythology or Christianity or whatever. But at the same time it connects to those stories, and if symbol is about anything it is about connection.

But aren't symbols and symbolism impossibly vague and hard to put a name on? Well, consider the cross, a no-smoking sign or something from a current TV advertisement. How strange and unfamiliar are those symbols? Because we are surrounded by symbols in everything from art to literature and street signs to advertising, why not allow ourselves to feel confident for a moment that we are not lost when it comes to them, or to their use, known as symbolism. We are talking about something familiar and indeed pervasive here. Let's not let the word put us off.

Back in the original Greek our word 'symbol' was originally two words. The first part *sym* or *syn* meant something like our English word 'together', and the second part came from the verb *bollo* which meant something like our English word 'throw'. So the word symbol means, approximately, to throw together or that which is thrown together. Therefore symbolism has to do with things which are thrown or put together. Two things, then, are brought together in a symbol.

But how did the word symbol come to have its present meaning? What is its history? One of the delights of etymology is discovering that even the most apparently conceptual words very often can be traced back to physical (tangible) objects. There was once an object called a symbol. It was usually a small round disk broken down the middle into two halves. The idea was to break the disk so that the two halves were jagged and uneven. This would ensure that no one else had a half symbol which would fit yours unless it was the original half. Two people then who had the two halves of a particular symbol could recognise each other – as, say, messenger and king – because their half symbols fit precisely together. Even if they had never met before, they could attempt to join half symbols and, if they fit, be pretty sure they were in the right company. Only these two, and no others, could combine to complete their particular symbol. It was unique to them and they were unique to it.

On their own, however, the two halves lacked that certain power. To try and boast of your half symbol would be like going about saying, 'Hey, I've got half the winning Lottery ticket! I want my prize.' It wouldn't count for much. For completeness, like fairy tale princes and princesses, halves need their other halves.

In a section on symbol in his *Living with Dreams*, Dr Roderick Peters offers the following reminder, if one were needed, of the prevalence of symbol in our lives.

> 'Artists of every kind learn about symbol; religious people of every religion learn about symbol; historians of culture learn about symbol; the advertising industry, including all propagandists, learn about symbol; some psychologists learn about symbol. Most of the remainder of society *experiences* symbol (on every poster, in every TV advertisement, for instance, as well as in every dream), is affected by it more or less unconsciously, but has learned little about it because it does not seem important enough.'

So, OK, symbol does seem to be something that is very important and widespread, but what does it have to do with telling stories? Well, for a start, someone who was to take some time out now and then and look at their own efforts at story not only might find out something about the characters involved, but also might occasionally discover something of interest about themselves.

But back again to our scene with John and Mary at the window. Let's think about that roll of film again. What if we were to change the roll of film to a bunch of photographic prints? What if John were to come in and find Mary going through his photographs? What difference would that have made? We could still tell the whole business about his having photographs hidden upstairs and hint that he has been having an affair, and all we'd lose is that silly image of the serpent at the end. There aren't even serpents in Ireland!

But it's not true that the scene would remain the same. For one thing, no scene exists solely on its own in a story; each has a relationship with what precedes and succeeds it. And each story even has a relationship to all the stories (about the same or even other characters) that the author might have chosen to tell.

More importantly, however, by switching to the photographs rather than the film, we've lost a huge amount of the suggestive power of this scene. And we've lost in the literal and in the mythological realms. A photograph is something that has been, literally, 'exposed'. John's secret is out. A roll of film on the other hand is, by definition, 'undeveloped'. Its contents are not yet out in the open. Indeed, they are in negative form, like a picture from another world. And that's exactly what they are. They are a view into the larger world of symbol where this story is running simultaneous to its running in the room at the window before us. The roll of film moving in the breeze has a life of its own. It is not something controlled by John, or by Mary, no matter how much either of them might try to control it. And the reader of this scene feels that the story has not ended here. For while Mary and John are static in their embrace by the window, the film, like a serpent, is moving.

At the end of the scene John might step on the serpent. Does he 'kill' it? Is the story coming towards its conclusion? Or does it slither away to rear its ugly head again later? If the latter, the symbol also helps to keep this story alive. It helps to keep a sense of danger in the story. It helps to maintain tension.

Equally, symbol can be a potent way of establishing resolution, or transition. John and Mary walk through a noisy, bustling city, but the author, like a camera operator, zooms in on a single bright flower pushing its way up through a crack in the pavement. Things are going to be all right. There will be growth.

And symbol doesn't have to be as hackneyed as I'm making it seem here. Nor does it belong only at the beginning and end of a story. In fact it can work anywhere. And many people contend that we can't draw on symbols when we please but that in fact *they* draw on *us, emerging* from our story-telling and poetry, and often when we least expect them. The poet Michael Longley in his poem 'The Pear; for John Montague' finds a pear and three oranges on the grave of Baudelaire and wonders if the pear is 'a symbol, a poetic windfall / a lucky sign' which his poem proves it to be. A writer cannot force a 'poetic windfall' to occur, but a good and practised writer learns to keep an eye open for the possibility.

And yet, even if it is hard to argue with the good sense of Wright Morris's assertion, 'When writing is good, everything is symbolic, but symbolic writing is seldom good,' let's see what happens were we consciously to go in search of them, were we to go out into the orchard, if you like, to shake a tree.

## PLAYING WITH SYMBOLS

Perhaps the best way to get better acquainted with symbols is to play a game with them.

1. Write down a list of 10 nouns describing objects in the physical world which have been in existence for at least 100 years. (My list might be door, tree, mountain, boat, wheel, bird, molecule, river, shit and ice. Or whatever.)

2. Next, imagine you are watching a sequenced film projection of these images. Door, tree, mountain ... What kind of music starts to play? Optimistic music, lonely music? With which object does the tone of the music change?

3. And now imagine that these pictures have been smuggled out of a prison in a country where feelings are banned? With his limited supply of pictures, what is the prisoner trying to tell you? What does he mean by 'door'? It's like trying to read Chinese ideographs. But he's trying to tell you a story. What is it about? It opens with a door and ends with ice. Do you think this is going to be a happy film? How about if it had opened with ice and then ended with the door? The differences are enormous.

4. In the third person singular (he went, she said, etc.), write a short story with no dialogue in which the 10 objects are encountered in sequence. (This is very similar to a game we played in the poetry section). Something like 'There was a man who sat all day before a door looking out at a single tree, etc.' Then try starting at the other end of the list and working backward.

5. For the main part of the game, now take each of these pictures (along with those vague shadows of narrative) and, viewing each as pure symbol, write a scene around it.

For convenience, in the beginning anyway, keep the scenes relatively short, no more than half a page or so. Somewhere there is going to be a door which seems to have almost unnatural presence or importance, a tree that may be in the background of the scene but which one of the characters is struck by, a mountain that someone is struggling to climb, a boat on a T-shirt of a child in a pram ... The objective here is not to hide these objects away in the scenes, but to place them in such a way that without being gaudy they attract attention. At all times they must be part of the story. (If there were no hidden love affair in the scene with John and Mary, that serpent roll of film might just become a roll of film after all. And, lest we give in to the temptation of having the breeze flip over the top page of Mary's ledger so that John can see the beginning of a note which reads *Darling Cuthbert, I shall be with you tomorrow and for ever ...*, we had probably better close that window altogether.)

So now, and taking your time at it, because in this game you have the opportunity to bring all of the fiction games so far into some level of play, begin. You have to make scenes which in some way focus on your ten objects in turn, but you also have to make scenes in which we see a slice of life. Therefore you will probably need some description of character and setting, some dialogue and maybe some exposition so we know what is going on. In short, you will need to pull together all of the strands we have been dealing with up to this point.

## CHANGING POINT OF VIEW

Often an interesting game to play with a scene or even a story as a whole, particularly if it feels like something is not quite working, is to experiment with switching about the point of view. For instance, a third-person narrative is told in the first person, or vice versa. Some things will work and others will suddenly make little sense, but often the switch around will offer you new possibilities for, or at least new insights into, the story.

Take, for instance, the famous opening of Franz Kafka's *Metamorphosis*, which I mentioned earlier, and let's see what happens when we change the third person to the first.

### Original Version

Gregor Samsa awoke one morning from uneasy dreams to find himself transformed in his bed into a giant insect.

### First-Person Version

I awoke one morning from uneasy dreams to find myself transformed in my bed into a giant insect.

Clearly the change of person, at least in this sentence, hasn't made a huge amount of difference to the meaning. But it has changed some of the possibilities of where this story will go and what it will be about. The fact that 'I' (Gregor Samsa) am now the narrator of the story, for a start, presupposes that I will not remain an insect very long, unless the story requires the reader to believe that an insect could be telling the story in the first place. In other words, a change like this, even in the opening sentence, greatly affects how this story *can* end. Second, it's going to make it at least a little harder for us to describe the physical details of Samsa's condition without recourse to a mirror or visitors who can speak or think about it, because I (Samsa) am unlikely to be able to view myself from all the angles in which the author could view me if I were set apart in the third person, set apart, in fact, like a third-person insect in a glass case.

At the same time, there are obviously advantages to be found in such changes of point of view. By making this change, it might prove to be much easier to get to understand Samsa's feelings and thoughts on his new condition (though Kafka manages to do this remarkably well anyway). Perhaps more importantly we would be forced into his mind and so have to view the events which befall him through his own eyes. This idea that we would have to take our version of the story from one of the people actually involved in it (in this case the central character) would also have a large effect on our reactions to the story. What if, for example, this new central character speaking in the first person were to tell us a bunch of lies? What if he were to be what is called an 'unreliable narrator'? 'I got up the other morning and found I was turned into a giant insect. No, only kidding, but my hangover made it feel like that.' Or: 'No, I didn't kill my wife. Honest. This blood on my hands? That's just, eh, ketchup. Really!'

This whole notion of switching to the voice of one of the characters in a story (and it could be a very minor character, not necessarily the central one) is interesting also for another reason. To some extent the author must be able to switch into her character's mind and voice if she is to know him well enough to make the story work. In fact, many people go so far as to conduct interviews with their characters, to ask them questions and write down their answers, in an effort to get to know what makes them tick.

## GRILLING THE SUSPECT

*'You can never know enough about your characters'*
– W Somerset Maugham

John loves Mary. Mary doesn't love John in return. John turns to Jane for help. Let's go back to that scenario again for a few minutes. Now when John gets to Jane's house and walks up to the door, just about to knock, I get stuck. My problem is that I don't know what John is going to say or do. I don't know if he's gone there happily ('Ah well, I'll ask Jane for help'), or whether somewhere inside him he feels this might not be a great idea. Clearly if John did have some kind of doubts, even the scene where he approaches the door (let alone the one where he actually talks to Jane) would become dramatic. But what kind of doubts *does* he have? Let's ask him.

John, what kind of doubts do you have?

John: 'I dunno. Doubts. What kinds are there?'

So you have doubts, it's just that you don't know what they are?

John: 'Yeah, like anybody else.'

And is that what frightens you?

John: 'What do you mean, frightens me? I'm not afraid. *What* am I afraid of? You think I'm afraid that Jane will reject my call for help? I think that's absolute rubbish.'

You think?

John: 'I know!'

And what about its opposite?

John: 'What do you mean its opposite?'

What if she does help? What if you do get Mary in the end? What then? What if she wants to marry you? What if she wants to turn you into a middle-aged family man? Did you ever wake up in the middle of the night sweating after a nightmare like that? 'As Gregor Samsa awoke one morning –'

John: 'No! What are you playing at? What are you trying to get me to say? That I'm secretly hoping Mary will reject me, or that Jane will reject me, and that I have some deep need to be rejected by women because of something that happened in my childhood? Look, I'm not interested in your amateur-psychologist approach to fleshing out your dramatic characters. Goodbye.'

What happened there? I took my own advice and tried to interview one of my characters (my main one, as it happens) and instead of learning anything I got told what I was doing was a waste of time. One of my own characters told me I couldn't write!

Actually, if you experiment with this idea of interviewing your characters, you'll find them telling you to buzz off with alarming frequency. After all, a character who has committed a murder will act pretty much like a real person who has committed a murder if you just walk up to him and start asking questions. To get to know a character, in a sense you have to allow that character to get comfortable in the interview. You have to play with your characters a little, particularly if you want them to talk about something they don't want to, or can't bring themselves to, talk about. And sometimes you can spend pages and pages talking to a character and in the end find nothing of all the material she offered amounts to anything or gets you any further.

Clearly, before we go near a character we need to have some idea of what we want to know. Let's say I suspect John has doubts but I want to get him to talk about them. I could go for the direct approach – 'John, you have doubts, don't you?' – but I probably wouldn't even get as far as I did above. Or I could guess that John had doubts but that, like most people, he probably won't want to discuss them with a relative stranger. To get him to open up I could try to find a way to approach the subject indirectly:

> You know, I admire you, John.
> John: 'Yeah? Why?'
> You've got guts. Marching up to Jane's door like this. That takes courage.
> John: 'Yeah, well ... I guess a little.'
> You guess?
> John: 'Well, OK, more than a little.'
> So, what do you think will happen?

OK, I've condensed this scene to the point where it's almost totally incredible, but the point I'm trying to make is that to get your characters talking you have to try to meet them halfway. You have to try to get them to relax and open up, to respond with feelings. Just asking them question after question is only likely to elicit a series of facts. Characters are not made of facts.

Coincidentally, just as I was typing up this section of the book I came across an article in the Sunday Review section of the *Independent on Sunday* newspaper in which psychiatrist

Dorothy Otnow Lewis interviews a man who has carried out the electric-chair executions of 19 people in the US. As 'Bob Smith' (not the man's real name) is either unwilling or unable to face the shocking situation of his own life, Otnow Lewis must find a way to guide him through territory he doesn't want to explore. Determined to find out more about a series of fights, beatings and even shootings in which the man was involved in his civilian life (in the hope that this will give her some glimpse into his psychic make-up), at one stage she asks him the question: 'Did you ever go further than you meant to?' She then follows this by telling her readers: 'That's a favourite question of mine. It's not just good with violent inmates. It's good with abusive parents. It helps them let you know what they've done to their kids without making them feel too guilty.' In a sense here, Otnow Lewis is showing us a way to conduct our own character interviews and suggesting that perhaps the best way to get the heart of the matter is to leave our tendencies to judge and condemn at least momentarily to one side.

As we've seen before, often by the time we come to an impasse in a story we will have spent some time thinking about that business of a character's home base and how her story will be the history of her movements off and back onto it. And if we know from this what the driving characteristics and desires and fears of our character are, then it seems logical to approach our interview with these in mind. When we talk about trying to get a character to open up, we mean in a way trying to get him to talk about where he is on that seesaw. If we think he is mad and upset, we should approach him gently. And if we think he is dreaming and deluded, maybe we should go in a little more dramatically. Not that we want to shock our characters, but we do want to provoke a response. The main problem with interviewing characters is that often they will only freely tell us what they want us to know, what we know already.

For some of us, this whole business will sound a little bit too New Age for our liking, interviewing characters who are only our own fingers on the typewriter. But that kind of reaction doesn't take from the fact that playing around like this is at least a way to develop the voices of our characters, to see what they sound like when their own words are written down, words we may never get to hear in the story proper because they don't belong there. That's what it can do, at least. At best it can also often help locate the driving energy of the story. While your conscious mind is concentrated on the business of writing down the two-part dialogue of the interview, you can often find yourself caught up in the scene and suddenly discover that your interviewee has said something really interesting. It might be a sudden, profound realisation on his part, or it might just be a slip of the tongue that he doesn't even seem to notice. But if plot comes from character, which it undoubtedly does, then it's back to character we have to go when we lose direction.

Before we move on to the next section, on climax, here are a few suggested questions one might try to ask of a character from any story.

📣

Experiment with your own ways of phrasing the following questions to elicit from your character what makes her tick.

1. What's your greatest strength?
2. What gets you into the most trouble?
3. Why do you do it if it gets you into so much trouble?
4. Who's in charge of your life? You? Are you in charge of *every* part of yourself or do you ever feel there are some parts that don't obey?

You can see how this line of questioning might go if we were lucky. *What gets you into trouble?* is a question that approaches the centre of the story? But *Why do you do it?* cuts straight to the heart, because in that answer will be a glimpse of the seesaw on which this particular character is balanced. Sometimes characters will even respond in an unexpected manner to questions, thereby proving Truman Capote's assertion: 'You can't blame a writer for what the characters say.' But authors cannot afford to accept powerlessness when it comes to trying to direct, provoke and draw out characters. 'The idea of authors running around helplessly behind their cretinous inventions,' said John Cheever, 'is contemptible.' But what's to be done with a character who just flails around pointlessly? As we discussed earlier in elementary plotting, it is now that we might introduce a second player who has himself a characteristic that will provoke our central character to act. Through this action our central character will reveal his weakness or strength, and the revelation of this weakness or strength will take place in the third section of drama which Aristotle attributed to plot: climax.

## CLIMAX

*'I write the ending first. Nobody reads a book to get to the middle'*
– Mickey Spillane

The climax is not the end of the story (despite the fact that non-writers often use it loosely to mean this), but it is the end of the plot. Once the climax is in place, all that is left to the author is to proceed towards the resolution of the story. And though this resolution might take up a considerable portion of the story's entire length, to a great extent its direction will already have been determined by the climax.

But one of the reasons why climax (our plot-based meaning) does still get confused with climax (the bit at the end where the hero kills the bad guy) is that in the plot-based climax, things can and very often do happen in a very physical way. Hamlet's killing of Polonius was not only dramatic and climactic, it was also our first glimpse of a drawn weapon in what proves to be a very bloody play indeed. When we get to the climax we should know we're approaching the climax; we should feel it; we should hear it. The climax is the fulcrum moment of the story. The last thing we want is to have our audience having to look back to see if they got it right.*Who was that behind the arras?* We want now to raise the level of excitement. We want readers to breathe faster. We shorten sentences. We appeal to the senses. We have as much movement as possible. Above all that came before, we want this scene to stand out.

If we were to draw up a climax checklist it might look something like this:

1. Has your central character got an emotional as well as a physical obstacle to try to overcome? Remember James Stewart in *Vertigo*. If he has, connect the two in the climax scene.*If the physical objective is small, the emotional one must be large.* It might only be a game of snooker, but if he loses they kill his girlfriend. Your central character*must* have something to lose.

2. Is there enough pressure on your central character? Time pressure (It's got to be done by Friday), responsibility pressure (By Friday or the kid dies), fear pressure (Eat the tarantula by Friday or the kid dies).

3. Have you shown through the story how the central character was driven? By desire? Fear? Ambition? Have we seen the central character's weakness and are we, at least somewhere in the backs of our minds, waiting for it to emerge? (If we don't already know James Stewart's character is afraid of heights, the belfry scenes in *Vertigo* are meaningless.)

4. Very importantly, and despite how the story might by times have seemed to force him to do things, is it clear that your character has a choice of behaviour (to do or to run, to kill or be killed), and therefore a dilemma?

5. Is the climax scene dramatic? What else can you bring to it by way of drama, energy, tension, danger? What else can you do with physical detail to make it striking and vivid?

6. If someone is excited their senses often dramatically improve. When you get the sudden frightening smell of smoke in your bedroom in the night, your eyes spring open, your ears suddenly seem to unclog. Your hands move in small fast motions. You speak in shorter sentences in times of action. What feelings does *your* scene convey? Does it look and sound active? Are you using punctuation to draw on the support of rhythm?

7. Has the 'villain' or the obstacle been bad or insurmountable enough? Is there anything else you can throw in to get the reader totally involved so that this one scene becomes crucial?

8. Have you paid attention to the symbolic levels of the scene and your character's actions in it?

---

Take your own climax scene, maybe the one you found earlier through the newspaper snippets, and explore it using the questions and suggestions in the list above.

In a sense, any of the above items might very usefully be checked in any scene of a story, if only to remind us that all scenes are in themselves miniature stories and will have their own moments of climax or maximum drama.

# RESOLUTION

After climax comes the resolution. John and Mary get together. Jane and John get together. Jane and Mary get together. No one gets together; the sad fact is a piano, which just happened to have been tied up outside John's window ... Either way, the story comes to its end and the climax will more or less have led you to the resolution. All you've really got to watch out for is attaching a little moral at the end. As Irwin Shaw says: 'The last paragraph in which you tell what the story is about is almost always best left out.' And, as protracted endings are not what this book is about, I'll keep this part very short. In fact, here it is in three fortune-cookie telegrams.

1. Get your climax as close to the start of your story as you can, then end the story as quickly as possible.
2. Beware the word 'suddenly'. Suddenly means the reader has had no expectation of, and therefore no feelings about, events to come.
3. When you've done all you can, quit while the going's good.

PS: I said a couple of pages back that climax doesn't mean the end of the story but the end of the plot. An obvious exception is Molly Bloom's soliloquy at the end of Joyce's *Ulysses*, a climax in every sense of the word. Which is a good place to finish. Yes, it is, yes.

# *Endgame*

## ADVICE FOR BEGINNING WRITERS

In order to open up this handbook to include approaches and opinions other than just my own, I invited a number of well-known writers to respond to a couple of questions, one of which was, *If you had any one piece of advice for beginning writers, what would it be?* Some of the writers whose responses follow have already been mentioned or quoted in the course of this handbook, and I should say their presence here does not necessarily mean they endorse my own methods or conclusions. However, I thought it would be interesting and informative for readers to see at a glance the differences *and* communality of their experience, and I'd like to thank all of these writers for taking the time to respond and for being willing and generous participants in what Eavan Boland calls 'the community of craft'.

*If you had any one piece of advice for beginning writers,*
*what would it be?*

**Michael Augustin** *poet*
'The Mission of Submitting Poetry to Poetry Magazines'

1. Make sure you send PLENTY of poems. Don't be bothered by any submission guidelines. Four or five will never do. Make it at least nineteen, or, even better, thirty-six. (What the heck: do send them all!)

2. Don't forget that editors don't really care about the poems. They always make their decision after reading your exciting cover letter. Tell them the story of your life! They can't wait to learn about your background; about all the prosaic hardship you suffered during your childhood, the wonderful schools and universities that shaped you!

3. Yes! Do tell them that all your poems are authentic! That they may appear odd but as a matter of fact are based on your very own experience! Go into detail! Give clues! Interpret your work! And don't forget to remind the editor, that you read some of the poems to your aunt and uncle on Christmas Eve and to some of your friends – who really, really liked them a lot!

4. Don't send the poems to the editorial address like everybody else does. Be smart. Try to get hold of the editor's private address and send them rrr-right there! Don't wait until you hear from him or her. Ring them up! Enquire! Leave a message with their wife or husband! Make use of the answering machine! Call again. What about six o'clock in the morning?

5. If you have followed my advice to this point – you'll probably never have any of your poems published in a poetry magazine. But your name will be well known among the editors. Guaranteed!

### Leland Bardwell *poet/novelist*

Women: Keep your nerve by avoiding literary assassination by your husband or partner. Strike out for independence. Lock yourself in the bathroom if necessary. Let the first sentence dance, so forget statement and polemic. You are your own woman and you have plenty to say. Read Roddy Doyle and at least one contemporary poem every day.

### Marvin Bell *poet*

Advice to beginners? Read something, then write something. Read something else, then write something else. Read like a thief. Understand that what is called originality is actually a mixture of influences. Do not try to avoid influence; seek it. Lose yourself in the materials. Welcome assignments, deadlines, and forms. Here is your mantra: Learn the Rules; Break the Rules; Make Up New Rules; Break the New Rules. Be not just willing to fail, but happy to. Understand that the bad stuff and the good stuff are all part of the stuff. Welcome the effects of time and dumb luck.

### Maeve Binchy *novelist*

The very best advice I ever heard was that first you choose a topic you know something about and then tell yourself in a very stern voice you MUST write ten pages a week. Not just hope to write ten pages or that you'll think about writing ten pages but that you MUST do it or else you will be prosecuted. Then in 30 weeks you will have a book. It may not be a good book but it will be a finished book and that will put you streets ahead of 99 per cent of the world.

### Eavan Boland *poet*

Chesterton's remark is a good one for workshops: 'If a thing's worth doing, it's worth doing badly.' The soundest advice for workshop writers is to bring in their worst work not their best, seize the help they get, and – most important of all – raise their tolerance level for their own failures.

**Dermot Bolger** *novelist/poet/playwright*

Writing is about re-writing, re-writing and re-writing. It's about running through the wall, the pain barrier when the words turn to muck in your mouth. It's about having the humility to recognise the flaws and start again, plus the arrogance to say I have something to say and I am going to say it. My first piece of advice to fiction writers is to get a good agent. My first piece of advice to poets is to rob a bank.

**Richard Caddel** *poet*

I used to think writing just came bang out of the skies perfectly formed, but it doesn't. You have to work at it, cutting out the abstract and the padding, shaping it so it sounds right, a well-made thing to last, not just for the moment. I still learn a lot by reading others – as widely and as diversely as possible – and by considering how they came to the noises they make – but mostly I learn by my own mistakes, by throwing away what doesn't stand up, by only believing in it when it's been road-tested to destruction. Workshops are OK if they're based on the trust of a group of people all in the same situation, but I wouldn't take – or ask for – the opinion of others, unless I knew their work thoroughly and could respect their words.

**Philip Casey** *poet/novelist*

Get publication out of your head. Write for your own pleasure. I published my first book of verse before I should have, and I regret that, but at least I had many years of innocence to wander about in my own soul. This is a great freedom which should be cherished. Publishing in small broadsheets or magazines can be invaluable after this period, as printing magically shows up flaws which a typescript doesn't. During this phase, leave work in a drawer for at least six months, preferably a year, to see if it still excites you as much as it did when you wrote it at three in the morning. Fortunately, I didn't publish my first novel till the age of 44, when I had a keen appreciation of just how hard it is to write well. It gets harder, thankfully.

### Billy Collins *poet*

To write is surely to be more alone than usual, but to write is also to join the varied company of other writers, both historic and contemporary. To write poetry is to join a Great Conversation consisting of nothing less than every voice that ever spoke in lines. But before making a contribution to that conversation, you need to know what has already been said, and to know the how of saying it. Therefore, read. Before painting a chair, sand it. Before writing a poem, read several hundred of them, several times. With a little luck, if you read widely and voraciously enough, you will discover a poet who makes you furious with jealousy. These objects of envy are sometimes referred to as 'mentors'.

### Evelyn Conlon *novelist*

Every *seanfhocal* has its contradiction: Absence makes the heart grow fonder; Out of sight, out of mind. So too with writing. Write what you know; Oh God, not again. But one thing for sure, you need to be prepared for a freefall of disappointment peppered with great moments of satisfaction. You may make a fortune, you may have to learn to live on a pittance. But if you are serious no one will stop you. No one will convince you that Lucien Freud was right when he said that a moment of complete happiness never occurs in the creation of a work of art. He said that promise of it is felt in the act of creation but disappears towards the completion of the work.

### Tony Curtis *poet*

If you have to write, at least take up reading poetry until you find what you like and dislike. From that wonderful position, you can at least be influenced or steal a few good ideas (which is advice I took long ago from an essay by TS Eliot). As to the actual writing of poems: sitting by a window or gazing out to sea, waiting for the muse to strike, might be a great pastime, but I believe you have to search for or hunt the poems in your own life. As Michael Hartnett says: 'I've poems at hand, it's words I cannot find.' You have to hunt for those words, those lines. Gary Snyder in his poem 'What You Should Know to Be a Poet' gives us a wonderful, magical list of all you should know. Then, close to the end of this extraordinary poem, he gives us the secret ingredient: 'work, long dull hours of work, swallowed and accepted ...' There is drink and madness in there somewhere, but most of the making of poems involves sweat, late nights and early mornings.

### John F Deane *poet/novelist*

Integrity! To aim for the highest possible standard by maintaining the integrity of one's beliefs, one's aspirations, one's commitment to the demands of form, and pursuing all of this in spite of disappointment and rejection.

### Greg Delanty *poet*

I suspect I'm not the only one to recommend here to beginning writers, or any writers at more advanced stages of beginning (which newcomers will be glad to know is all of us), that reading poetry for an hour or so daily is simply essential and for so many reasons: enjoyment, nourishment, learning different techniques of style, etc. For prose writers they should be reading as much prose. Both types of writers should read poetry and prose on a regular basis. If the writer of poems doesn't read poetry then the writer's obituary might read something like 'Obituary of a Poet Who Never Read Poems': 'All his scribbling life he tried to write awesome, eternal verse / Alas, he's his own last rejection slip, fastpost now in a hearse.'

### Michael Dibdin *novelist*

1.  Don't write about what you know. It's much less interesting than you think.
2.  Above all, don't write about yourself. Everyone is much less interesting than they think.
3.  Don't flaunt your recondite vocabulary, ability to juggle multiple subordinate clauses, knowledge of foreign languages, etc. Nobody likes a smart-arse.
4.  Actually, books should be written to give pleasure to the reader, not to you.
5.  Don't hesitate to portray all the bastards you know in intimate detail. It will liven things up no end and they never recognise themselves.
6.  Write the book first and do the research afterwards. You'll need much less than you think.

7. If you can't get started, write the first and last scenes as short stories, then join them up in unexpected and intriguing ways.

8. No dream sequences, please.

9. Books are a game between writer and reader. As when playing golf with your boss, make sure the reader wins.

10. Viable fiction requires memorable characters and a sense of purposeful momentum. If these continue to elude you, there's always poetry.

11. It's very easy to stop reading, and easier still never to start. At the end of every MSS page, ask yourself why the reader should bother to keep going. Don't do so yourself until you have a satisfactory answer to this question.

12. Your determination, industry and unshakeable belief in your genius are indeed admirable, but don't give up the day job just yet.

### Gerard Donovan *poet/novelist*

I'd say that the advice I'd have for beginners really has five steps:

1. Read and study modern and contemporary short stories/novels/poetry (including quality lit mags);

2. Learn basic literary terms such as character, plot, metaphor, image, scene, motivation, setting, etc. and understand how they can relate to one's own creative work;

3. Study Aristotle's three unities (place, time and action) in order to give stories realistic frameworks, or in the case of poetry, learn some poetic forms (sestinas, villanelles, etc.) as a way of generating content;

4. Take advantage of the peer review system that workshops offer by submitting work that needs polishing ...

5. Understand the difference between literary fiction or poetry and confessional autobiography/journal work. Beginning writers are usually emotionally connected to their work and often take criticism personally.

Finally, I never allow the writer whose work is under review to speak until the process is over. Writers should avoid responding to comments unless directly invited – it's a no-win situation.

### Katie Donovan *poet*

[In the ideal workshop] everyone is committed to making honest but constructive suggestions as to how to improve a piece of writing under discussion (concentration is vital, and taking notes greatly aids the process). And the one piece of advice? Find your own voice and trust it.

### Roddy Doyle *novelist/screenwriter*

Don't be in a hurry. Time is the most effective editor. What seemed like a glorious piece of work will, more times than not, be less impressive when read three days, weeks, months later. You may find five sentences where you only needed one. You had to write the first four to get to the vital one. Given time to calm down, you will recognise the flabbiness of the first four sentences and give them the old red biro treatment, leaving you with the one great sentence. Then you're finished.

### John Dunne *novelist*

Tentative commandments: 1) Read; 2) Write about what you don't know; 3) Please only yourself; 4) Don't be tyrannised by meaning; 5) Listen to the rhythm; 6) Declare war on adjectives; 7) No novel should exceed 300 pages; 8) The prime purpose of fiction is confrontation; 9) Social realism belongs to newspapers; 10) If you're still in a writers' group after three years, give up.

### Peter Finch *poet*

One of the hardest things in writing is making the space in which to do it. No one can turn the poems well between phone calls, visits, conversations and disturbances. There's the idea at the top of your head and then the window cleaner knocks demanding his £3 for making the glass once again like air. He tells you it's a fine day and you agree. You both look at the clouds and then you hunt around for the cash to settle his bill. By the time you get back that idea of yours has fallen over, altered irrevocably or can simply no longer be remembered. You try to start again but all you can think about is the state of that window cleaner's shirt. A novelist might put that shirt into the current chapter but for the poet it isn't that simple. The poet needs protected hours – time alone – and the will to stay inside them. I fixed it for me by marking out one day a week during

which there would be no interruptions, ever. I told everyone I didn't hate them and was not being rude just sensible, plugged in the answer machine, took the batteries out of the door bell, told the children to bother someone else today with their home-work queries, locked the study door, turned on the processor and let the music flow. It took an hour or so to get into the swing but the idea worked. It was difficult, turning down work on that day, refusing medical appointments and visits by men to repair my loose slates and leaking radiators. Can't come, I'd say, I won't be here. Writers might be convivial souls and to be any good they need to be fond of the world but to write they need to love loneliness. At the end of the day writing is a thing you do best on your own.

### Janice Fitzpatrick Simmons *poet*

Beginning writers tend to present poems they are convinced are finished poems. This defeats the purpose of the workshop which is to find the poem in its infancy and help it along the path it needs to take. Be open to change and read as many poets (Irish, American, English and poets in translation) as you can.

### Eamon Grennan *poet*

Something I often notice is a superabundance of metaphor, so the lines get clogged. In other words, 'poeticality'. A recent piece had 'tiara of stars', 'thigh of the breeze' and 'pyramid of eyes' in the space of five short lines. That 'of' construction can be a damager too, if overdone. The less is more principle applies here. Another common thing is being too 'gnomic' – making an image that has no hook into the context. Sounds good in itself, but goes nowhere. Another is not having much sense of why a line might break, so the ear isn't very developed as far as the unfolding of the line-by-line music of a piece is concerned. And one piece of advice? Read more – expand the taste for other poets. Love the language. Trust plainness. (That's three pieces, no matter.) The good workshop, I guess, really depends on sensing the peculiarity, in every sense, of each writer, so general strictures or suggestions probably only have a limited use or value.

### Dermot Healy *poet/novelist*

You are not as good as you think you are, you're worse, but one thing is – if you keep hacking away you'll finish one day whatever it is you started out with. Working every day helps with the novel. Don't tell too much about characters on the first page. Keeping a notebook, getting up early, listening helps. Just because a thing really happened does not mean it will work in fiction. Sentence making is by its nature a form of illusion. You are always editing. When you read an author, read all belonging to them. Put your new poems away for a few months or years. There's no need to hurry into print. All the above are irrelevant in a way because there are no set rules. And what rules there are you'll break to get your own voice motoring. And then you'll find you are not unique. It's language is.

### Seamus Heaney *poet/playwright*

Beginning to write – especially if you are to be a poet – is not like beginning to drive or beginning to ride a bike. Composition is not a skill learnt once and for all, then lodged with you forever. No matter how 'experienced' you become as a poet, every time you start on a piece of new work you are as tentative, as apprehensive and as liable to chance and failure as you were the first time. Nobody can ever tell you how exactly they succeeded in writing the poems they believe in, so nobody can tell you how to write the ones you will have to believe in. My advice, therefore, is about reading rather than writing: keep reading those poets who bring you to life, the ones who excite you enough to make you want to write. That awakened mood is the *sine qua non* at any stage of development.

### Christopher Hope *novelist*

For me writing is a form of fear-management. Fear of the blank page, fear of the unknown. But that's good. It keeps you concentrated, on edge. And the only way I can still the fear is by pushing forward into it, shaping it, making it better. Quite what is made better, I don't know but the relief is amazing. I think those who take to the deeply odd trade of writing probably lack some crucial component. Writing is a result, and a way of remedying this. It stabilizes, somehow.

### Bernard MacLaverty *novelist*

One of the best pieces of advice is Flannery O'Connor's 'All fiction is a series of pictures.' I don't know where it comes from (I'd be grateful for a reference). It stops people writing essays or thoughts. It is also a way of describing the 'telling' and 'showing' distinction. Also in this vein I like Willa Cather's 'What is expressed on the page but never named.' Forgive me, these are not quotations but approximations.

### Maighread Medbh *performance poet*

Be brave, don't be afraid to experiment. Deconstruct, deform, play around. Scour the bookshops, find something you like and imitate it. Follow sounds and pictures. Say it exactly as you experience it. Don't try to be acceptable at first or you might never get the chance to rebel. Take it one minute at a time. Even when not yet published, keep writing, there's nothing else. Your friends will love your work. Enjoy that but never believe them. If you have even the slightest doubt, re-write because doubts, like dreams, are real messages and they're usually right.

### Paula Meehan *poet/playwright*

Listen to all advice but don't follow any that doesn't make sense to your deepest instinct and that you feel literally in your bones, no matter how big the reputation of the advisor, or how much you love them. Poetry needs the wayward children as much as the well behaved. You're mapping the wilderness – go wild. Also mind the body. Eat. Sleep. And learn the craft so the art can root and be earthed.

### Paul Muldoon *poet*

One piece of advice for beginning writers? Write one line at a time. Try to get it right as you go along. Don't feel compelled to get it all down. If it's of interest it's not going anywhere. This doesn't mean that one never goes back to revise. Only that the more attention one gives as one goes along the less need there'll be to go back and repoint that brick at the foot of the wall.

**Joseph O'Connor** *novelist/playwright*

I don't do any teaching or workshop-leading myself. But I think the main problem of most writers' early work, including my own, is a tendency to write like somebody else. The hardest, most frustrating and time-consuming thing any writer has to do is find her or his own voice. After that comes the admittedly difficult but much more possible task of learning the technical skills of narrative, image, pace, character development, etc. But there's no point in trying to learn them if you don't really know what you're going to do with them.

The other thing I would say is this: at some point, all beginning writers are given the advice 'write about what you know'. I think that's terrible advice. It stops people using their imaginations. My own view is that writers should write about what they feel and sense and imagine to be true, not about what they know to be. [And one piece of advice?] My advice would be to write! Don't natter about what you are going to do; instead, do it. Write, write and then write some more. Make writing a part of your life by making it a part of your day, your evening, your week, your weekend, whatever you can afford. Fix a regular time in which you write and rigorously stick to that. Tell your friends, loved ones, children, that this is something you do in that time, that it is important to you and that during that time you will not be available to do other things. So many writers, whether they are beginners or established names, waste so much time by far too much talking and thinking and dreaming about writing. Do not worry, at first, about getting it right. Ju get it written. And then you can begin to fix it.

**Andrew O'Hagan** *novelist*

A novelist should know when to say nothing, because knowing when to say nothing is evidence of the novelist's tact. It may also be the hallmark of his style and a way for the reader to live inside the quality of the narrative. Too many new novelists appear to know very little about their characters: really, you should know everything about them, down to the dreams they might have. The good novelist knows his characters' way of coping (or not coping) with life, and he knows something large about the society they live in too. One might carefully, delicately, riskily, put these things in play in writing a novel,

but it will come to nothing if the language is not exact. Life is not arithmetic – there is no single solution – but a good novel should nevertheless command the force of its own moral maths in order to be beautiful.

### Mary O'Malley *poet*

Read more and more – and trust your instincts. That to older writers even more!

### Jane Urquhart *novelist*

My first piece of advice to an aspiring writer would be to maintain a healthy scepticism toward all rules, all creative writing classes and all disseminators of advice, including (and maybe especially) yours truly.

That being said, there are two things that I know for sure a writer can't live without, and those two things are unstructured time, on the one hand, and, as V Woolf has already told us, a room of one's own on the other.

Picture this room. Do you see anyone other than the writer lolling about on the bed in the corner, or perched at the desk in front of the window? Do you see gossiping friends or demanding relatives? No you do not, for the simple reason that while one is writing it is essential that one be alone.

So my second (or is it my third?) piece of advice to an aspiring writer would be to make solitude your friend, and if solitude is not your friend (i.e. if you hate being alone) then give up writing altogether. If you choose this world you are going to be spending a great deal of time alone in it. This does not necessarily mean that you should flee to a beehive hut on the Greater Skellig Island, but you must give yourself at least an opportunity to remain apart, both in spirit and in flesh, so that the work can grow in your mind.

### Eamonn Wall *poet*

Buy a notebook, a small one will do, and carry it around with you, and write in it as often as you can.

## Marina Warner *novelist*

[The most common problem?] An unwillingness to invent, to imagine, to fabricate and to observe others. The contemporary strength of memoirs, confessions and, in general, the autobiographical mode leads many writers to believe they must explore their own histories and past, instead of infusing made up, borrowed or even traditional, old stories with personal experience. [And one piece of advice?] Practise! And read! Writing is like singing, and you can't find your pitch or control your expression unless you do your scales and warm up your chords, daily, and listen to others and the way they do it.

And finally, if I may, to add the words of the American short story writer William Saroyan: 'The most solid advice to a young writer is this, I think: try to learn to breathe deeply, really to taste food when you eat, and when you sleep, really to sleep. Try as much as possible to be wholly alive, with all your might, and when you laugh, laugh like hell, and when you get angry, get good and angry. Try to be alive. You will be dead soon enough.'

What kind of books and reference materials might be useful in a writer's library or might a writer do well to have a look at? What kind of books might a writing group do well to pool their resources to buy? We've already seen that many of the books most useful for the beginning or practising writer are not all about writing *per se*. Books on body language, dictionaries of quotations, etc. all have their value for the writer who is looking for new kinds of stimulation. What follows is a very personal round-up of some of the books that might be useful, most of them from my own alarmingly expanding collection of reference works. While one or two of these might catch your fancy, we should all try to remember that the very best guides to creative writing, poetry or fiction are works of poetry and fiction themselves. In fact, once one has worked through the suggested games and exercises in a book like this, the next step is to go back to those books of poetry and fiction that have most impressed you over the years and, armed with (I hope) a new confidence and openness, re-read them to see what it was that so impressed you. We can sit around until kingdom-come talking about what poems or stories are or can be, but the best way to understand what they are is to read them and, particularly with poems, to read them aloud.

Meanwhile, here are some books that have been mentioned earlier or that you might find inspiring.

### General Reference

*The Compact Oxford English Dictionary*, if you can afford it, or justify it to yourself, is irresistible: the whole of the OED in a single volume (each page has nine pages of the original reproduced on it, and there are 2,386 pages in the book, which makes a whopping 21,474 reproduced pages). With almost 300,000 entries, comprehensive etymologies and two and a half million quotations, there's nothing to beat it. Unless perhaps the same thing on CD. Still Chambers produce great desk dictionaries, and Wordsworth Reference publish one of them in a very cheap paperback as their *Concise English Dictionary.*

*Roget's Thesaurus,* Peter Mark Roget. Available in a huge number of editions, Roget's is one of the few books that every writer should have. Not only a handy reference for finding that elusive word, but also an extraordinary classification of everything from the physical world to emotions and abstract thought. Don't be tempted by the simpler-looking A-Z works on the market.

*Dictionary of English Etymology,* Walter W Skeat, Wordsworth Reference. A famous work on the origins and development of the English language, Onions' being the other famous one. Skeat's dictionary is full of fascinating family trees and unexpected linkages sure to tantalise any writer or poet.

### Poetry

*The Art and Craft of Poetry,* Michael J Bugeja. A step-by-step approach to the techniques of poem-making, clearly written and with many fine examples, though the neat breakdown of poetry into genres and types is a little irritating.

*Writing Poems,* Peter Sansom, Bloodaxe Books. Poem structures, metre, rhyme, etc., all examined and clearly explained with plenty of examples. A limited number of exercises too, but better as a text book.

*Writing Poetry, and Getting Published,* Matthew Sweeney and John Hartley Williams, Teach Yourself Books. Clear, witty and provocative, like the poems of the two authors themselves, this is a very welcome book full of insights and examples.

*The Poet's Manual and Rhyming Dictionary,* Frances Stillman. An indispensable handbook on poetic form and metre, with a very clear and useful rhyming dictionary. Examples of work tend to be taken from the English 'cannon' that frightened so many of us away from poetry in school but, if you can cope with that, a fine addition to any poet's library.

## Fiction

*Writing for Your Life*, Deena Metzger, Harper San Francisco. Fascinating journey through myth, personal history and games. One of the very best writing books available.

*Writing Down the Bones*, Natalie Goldbert, Shambala. The other classic writing handbook. 'Unlearning' rather than 'learning' is Goldbert's preoccupation, but the book has far more edge, wit and flair than this simple synopsis would suggest.

*The Handbook of Short Story Writing*, Vols. 1 and 2, ed. Jean M Fredette, Writers Digest. To-the-point essays on various aspects of short story writing – plot, dialogue, climax, etc. – by major American writers. Well worth having.

*The Art & Craft of Novel Writing*, Oakley Hall, Story Press, USA. Excellent book on structure and techniques of novel writing, most of which is of equal interest to short story writers. All the better for the way in which Hall draws on extensive quotations from well-known and recent fiction to illustrate his points.

## Plot

*The Thirty-Six Dramatic Situations*, Georges Polti. A book written in a strangely abbreviated language which breaks down the possibilities of plot into 36 basic situations (telling us even Schiller couldn't find more): Supplication, Deliverance, Crime Pursued by Vengeance, etc. Sadly, many of the examples referred to are obscure or out of print, but the book does certainly inspire thought.

*Playwrighting, How to Write for the Theater*, Bernard Grebanier. Though obviously concerned with stagecraft, the chapters on plot and structure are fascinating and very well explained. The author does have a tone which might fairly be described as 'opinionated', but then maybe that kind of challenge is just what many of us need.

### Body Language

*Teach Yourself Body Language*, Gordon R Wainwright, Teach Yourself Books. Deceptively simple analysis of body language and body customs, complete with illustrations and fascinating insights.

### Quotations

*A Dictionary of Contemporary Quotations*, Jonathon Green, Pan Books. It may be unfair to single out one dictionary of contemporary quotations for attention, but Green's is fascinating because it shows his sense of humour and play, qualities not always evident in such collections.

*Scorn*, Matthew Parris, Hamish Hamilton Ltd. Anthology of discourtesy, disparagement, invective, ridicule etc. Very funny. Bristling with possibilities.

### Symbols

*The Penguin Dictionary of Symbols*, John Chevalier and Alain Gheerbrant, Penguin. Brilliantly researched if a little dense.

*The Wordsworth Dictionary of Symbolism*, Hans Biedermann, Wordsworth Reference. Originally published in English by Facts on File Inc., New York, Biedermann's paperback is learned, packed with information, readable and, like all the Wordsworth titles, amazingly cheap.

*A Dictionary of Symbols*, Tom Chetwynd, Paladin. Another dictionary written in a strangely abbreviated style which, if you can get used to it, will repay casual browsing or focused research. Wide-ranging and well cross-referenced.

### Dreams

*Dictionary for Dreamers*, Tom Chetwynd, Paladin. An excellent book. Chetwynd doesn't try to explain dreams, which is where so many of his competitors come undone, but helps the reader to make the connections between symbols and their common and personal meanings.

### WEB LINKS

In recent years the World Wide Web has evolved into a major and sometimes even reliable resource for information on all aspects of writing and publishing. As links go out of date all the time or lead to dead ends, undoubtedly the best place to begin looking is on the web itself, but following are a few tried-and-trusted sites, both worth a look in themselves and useful as springboards, or surfboards, to further exploration.

As geographical proximity is often of little concern to the web user, I'll list just a few 'national' organisations and resources first, beginning with the nearest-to-hand, and then concentrate on sites that specialise in particular aspects of the literary and publishing world.

*(For convenience, all of the listed web addresses, and many more, are included on the links page of the author's web site,* www.patboran.com.*)*

### Geographical

**Poetry Ireland** *www.poetryireland.ie*
Ireland's national poetry organisation. Information on poets, poetry, readings, workshops. Publishes a quaterly magazine, *Poetry Ireland Review,* and a bi-monthly newsletter, *Poetry Ireland Newsletter,* also available in pdf format.

**Irish Writers' Centre** *www.writerscentre.ie*
Info on readings, workshops and other events. Many links and a newsletter (pdf available) on writing-related matters.

**Irish Writers Online** *www.irishwriters-online.com*
Extensive biographical Dictionary of Irish Writers maintained by poet and novelist Philip Casey.

**Poetry Society** *www.poetrysociety.org.uk*
The UK Poetry Society's site includes info on events and programmes, and highlights and excerpts of the society's flagship *Poetry Review.*

**Poets & Writers Inc.** *www.pw.org*
US magazine with news on publishing and markets. The Classifieds section, accessible on the web site, includes details of US journals currently seeking submissions.

**Academy of American Poets** *www.poets.org*
Extensive biographical material on American poets, including a nationwide events calendar (less than extensive), links to poems in text and audio formats and a video and CD gift shop.

**Peter Finch** *www.peterfinch.co.uk*
As good as a national poetry institution, the UK's Peter Finch maintains a homepage which includes regularly updated info and links for poets and writers.

**The Poetry Kit** *www.poetrykit.org*
One of the best UK poetry sites, founded by the late Ted Slade, the Poetry Kit includes information on competitions and festivals, national and international magazines and outlets, an events calendar and links to audio sites.

## Creative Writing Courses

*Poets & Writers* lists 323 'writing programs' in the US alone, and there are likely many more smaller ones not listed. The choice is so vast that you have to talk to someone who's completed one before even considering it, and as well as college-based MFA and other programmes, many arts and literature centres run short and long-term poetry, fiction and non-fiction courses. For residential, short-term courses in Ireland and the UK, the following provide a wide range of options:

**Dingle Writing Courses** *www.dinglewritingcourses.ie*
In the inspirational setting of the Lios Dana centre, which overlooks the magnificent three-mile strand of Inch, Co. Kerry, Ireland, these residential writing courses are conducted by some of the best-known Irish and international poets and writers.

**Arvon Foundation** *www.arvonfoundation.org*
Taking place 'over four-and-a-half days at residential writing centres in Devon, Shropshire, Yorkshire and Inverness-shire', the Arvon Foundation's highly respected courses include all aspects of writing from poetry, short fiction and genre fiction to song writing and writing for radio and TV.

## Audio/Visual

**Lannan Foundation** *www.lannan.org*
This American foundation not only financially supports writers and writing in many ways but also has built up huge audio and video resources featuring writers reading from and discussing their work. Much of this material

(for which you'd do well to have a broadband or similar high-speed connection) is now available on line.

**Electronic Poetry Centre** *http://wings.buffalo.edu/epc*
Great resource including home pages of poets, biographical info and even some sound files.

**Poetry Jukebox** *www.poetryjukebox.com*
UK-based 57 Productions' growing collection of audio poetry with a simple-to-navigate, attractive interface.

### Essays & Fine Writing

**Arts & Letters Daily** *www.aldaily.com*
A real contender for the best literary site on the web, Arts & Letters Daily provides constantly updated links to first-class literary articles available in hundreds of online journals and print periodicals, making it a virtual broadsheet of excellent and stimulating writing.

### eBooks
**Project Gutenberg** *www.gutenberg.net*
Enormous resource for electronic texts (ebooks) in downloadable Plain Text format.

**The Internet Classics Archive** *http://classics.mit.edu*
English literature classics on the net.

**Internet Public Library** *www.ipl.org*
Alphabetised, categorised and browsable links to many thousands of reference and literary resources.

### eZines
A small number of print journals and magazines maintain really comprehensive web sites (for obvious commercial reasons), while the majority of eZines in fact exist only in the digital domain. Some are married to a

publishing house, and in essence bridge the gap between publication catalogue and sampler, while others embrace the new technology in more experimental, sometimes even radical ways.

**Jacket** *www.jacketmagazine.com*
Australian poet John Tranter's highly respected quarterly online magazine of 'poetry and creative prose' with an ever-expanding archive.

**2River** *www.2river.org*
US poet Richard Long's excellent online publishing house, since 1996 issuing fine new work in html, pdf and more recently in print formats.

**Electric Acorn** *http://acorn.dublinwriters.org*
Ireland's original online literary journal where visitors from all over the world can respond to the published work. See also parent site, Dublin Writers' Workshop, www.dublinwriters.org.

### Daily Poems

There are quite a few lists which send their subscribers a daily poem or other digital text. These are among the best:

**Poetry Daily** *www.poems.com*
A great resource for what's going on in the poetry world. If you haven't already done so, sign up for the free newsletter.

**Poem of the Day** e-mail *nastasios.kozaitis@verizon.net*
Not to be confused with the site above, Poem of the Day is in fact a free daily e-list maintained by Queen's, NY-based poet Anastasios Kozaitis. If you appreciate someone taking the time to send you, free and every single day, whatever poem has happened to connect with him that day, then you'll be dropping him a polite request to join the list and expecting everything from

Auden to Zukofsky with some real surprises in between.

## And finally, a word of caution for poets

**Poetry.com** *www.poetry.com*
Misremembering or mistyping the URL for the excellent Poetry Daily or Academy of American Poets sites (listed above) could lead you to this less-than-inspiring site which recently trumpeted its plans to award no less than '1175 prizes totaling (sic) $58,000.00 to amateur poets in the coming months'. If headlines like this don't make you just a little bit nervous, and suspicious, maybe poetry is not really for you after all.

# Select Bibliography

Boran, Pat. 'Penknife' from *As the Hand, the Glove* (Dedalus, 2001); excerpt from 'Stars', originally published in *The Honest Ulsterman/The Southern Review* (US); excerpt from 'Letters to the Dead' originally published in *WP Monthly* and *The Letter Box*; a version of 'Bats in the Belfry' originally appeared in *The Waterford Review*.

Collett, Peter. *The Book of Tells*. Doubleday, London, 2003.

De Bono, Edward. *The Use of Lateral Thinking*. International Center for Creative Thinking, 1967.

Houchin, Ron. 'To the Woods'. By permission of the author.

Hugo, Richard. *The Triggering Town*. WW Norton & Company Inc., New York, 1979.

Neruda, Pablo. 'Some Thoughts on Impure Poetry' from *Passions and Impressions*. Trans. Margaret Sayers Peden. Farrar Straus & Giroux, New York, 1983.

O'Driscoll, Dennis. *Troubled Thoughts, Majestic Dreams: Selected Prose Writings*. Gallery Press, Loughcrew, 2001.

Peters, Roderick. *Living with Dreams*. André Deutsch Limited, London, 1990.

Stillman, Michael B. 'Lying in the Field' from *In an Eye of Minnows* by Michael Stillman. Copyright © 1976 by Michael Stillman.

Virgilio, Nicholas A. 'On the cardboard box ...' from *Selected Haiku*, Second Edition, augmented by Nicholas A Virgilio. Burnt Lake Press, USA, 1988.

Wyley, Enda. 'Wedding Gift' from *Eating Baby Jesus*, Dedalus Press, Dublin, 1994.

# Index